INDEX

Part 1

THE RISE OF SOCIALISM IN AMERICA

I am writing this book because of the love that I have for these United States of America. A nation that was truly formed by its people and for the people, with a sincere and honest approach to govern the people of this nation in a fair and just manner. Laws carefully written to ensure the citizens of this great nation, that justice would be distributed equally to all.

Our forefathers gave us a Constitution and a Bill of Rights. These great men in our past, came together when there was need to guide a new nation on a path to a true form of freedom, not ever realized in this world before. It was laid out very clearly. A fair and balanced form of government with checks and balances that protected and served the will of the people of this new nation, not that of the government.

Our government was to be the tool for the citizens of this great nation, to work the will of the majority of the people. Our government gave us these laws that would guide us, to maintain a free and fair nation for its citizens, and were regardless of race, creed or nationalities, with religious freedom for all.

1

These values that our forefathers put forth guaranteed that our government would remain small, so that the people could grow without the restraints of government. The intention was that all humans are created equal, *that they are endowed with unalienable rights, and that among these are life, liberty and the pursuit of happiness.*

This idea of a free nation resonated throughout most of the world. As of 1787, people have been flocking to this country with dreams of freedom and prosperity to this present day. They were seeking a path to citizenship in a belief that freedom could be attained, to be part of a nation that would enable them to grow and prosper to enjoy a way of life that they could never have realized, because no other nation has ever extended this form of freedom to its people before.

It was clear to the men and women that came here, that only through hard work and a strong effort could they achieve their goals. This to them was not realized as a burden, but a privilege. That to be able to have the freedom of speech, to express their thoughts without being oppressed, is a God given right that should be realized by all nations of this world.

Be able to travel unburdened throughout the great states of these United States, made them realize, that the pursuit of happiness was at their fingertips.

That true freedom could become a reality, had a humbling effect that united the people that came to America even more.

The greatness of this country was realized by the people that came to America, mostly in past wars that were fought on the soil of this nation and in the land of wherever our allies were threatened.

It was realized, when the woman of this nation took on the jobs of the men, that went off to war to fight. Rosie The Riveter stands out as an inspirational icon to the women of this work force. It was remarkable to see how this country came together, become united, the likes of which, was never seen before.

During the second World War, it was realized in work places and in the factories across this land. It was realized in shops producing guns and ammunition. It was realized in the automobile industry where cars manufacturing changed to producing jeeps, army trucks, tanks, fighter planes and bombers, all in record numbers.

Shipyards of this nation, like all other work forces in America, were busy around the clock. Every Sea Port on our coastlines from the Atlantic Ocean to the Pacific Ocean were working nonstop for twenty-four hours a day, seven days' a week turning out ships of different types and classes.

The entry of the United States into the war in late 1941 injected financial, human and industrial resources into Allied operations. Like the Commonwealth countries, the US produced more than its own military forces required and armed itself and its allies for the most industrialized war in history. At the beginning of the war, the British and French placed large orders for aircraft with American manufacturers and the US Congress approved plans to increase its air forces by 3,000 planes.

In May 1940, Franklin D. Roosevelt called for the production of 185,000 airplanes, 120,000 tanks, 55,000 anti-aircraft guns and 18 million tons of merchant shipping in two years. Adolf Hitler was told by his advisors that this was American propaganda; in 1939, annual aircraft production for the US military was less than 3,000 planes.

By the end of the war US factories had produced 300,000 planes, and by 1944 had produced two-thirds of the Allied military equipment used in the war—bringing military forces into play in North and South America, the Caribbean, the Atlantic, Western Europe and the Pacific. We were able to supply our allies and our own fighting forces on land and at sea, with an endless amount of food, equipment and supplies. That continued to the end of the war.

It was there for the rest of the world to see how magnificent this great nation was and how quickly it could gain the strength needed to face any crises that arose.

A war machine was developing at home, so huge, so powerful, and so wide spread throughout this land, that it made us, the United States of America, the greatest and largest power that ever existed on this earth.

It gave credence to the word united, it was a proud nation of people, young and old of many different ethnic back grounds, that came together to minimize the grief and struggle that wars can bring.

It made the men and women and the children of this great nation proud to be an American. And proud they were, patriotism was utmost in the minds of all that lived in this great country, the United States of America.

It was shortly before the second world war, it appeared, that changes in our government started to take place. It reflected in our educational system.

Our schools throughout America were being introduced to a new idea in the method that our students were to be taught.

In our schools, along with subjects like Math,

English, History and others, there was a class called Current Events.

Abruptly, a few weeks into the beginning of a new term, that name changed from Current Events to Social Studies, not realizing the effect of what was the beginning of the effort to reshape America.

Our teacher's at the time, taught us this new class in a way that tried to minimize the greatness of American history. For months thereafter, all we heard was how bad and unfair our Constitution and the Bill of Rights were. They would make comparison examples of our law to the laws of other nations.

They would especially glorify socialist nations when doing so. It was the start to capture the minds of the youth of America. To transform them to become the future socialist in the years to come.

Liberals started to become the new generation of teachers in our schools. Our American history classes gradually started to change. There were fewer lessons of American history now being taught.

The lessons in our American history class, over a period of a few weeks diminished to a point where there was none at all. It slowly became a history of world events that were taught in class.

We were told that this change over to Social Studies from Current Events is an advanced form of education. It is called the progressive system of education. This changeover was taking place in all the schools across the nation.

As children we were not concerned with or understood what was really going on, we just accepted this new class being taught to us. This new program was introduced unchallenged. No one had any idea, at that time, of how it might affect the educational system of our country. However, the effects were profound.

It was many years later that what was really taking place back then, was clearly explained in a book I read called, "NON DARE CALL IT TREASON" by John A. Stormer. His book was about the dangers of Communism and the cancerous Progressive Movement taking hold in the political parties of our Government.

When Japan attacked us in Pearl Harbor, the lesson's that slandered our Constitution abated, not to arise its head again till after the second world war ended. Our schools, at that time, were rated number one in the world – today, we're rated at number twenty-six and falling.

Change in our government may have started in the late thirties, but the change really may have begun with Mrs. Eleanor Roosevelt in the years of 1900 to 1918. It was a political organization founded in Britain on January 4, 1884 with the main purpose of bringing about socialism to Britain, Europe, the United States of America and eventually to the rest of the world.

A plan was formulated by a group of men and women, with the idea that nations can be taken over by gradual and lawful means rather than by revolutions and devastating, destructive wars.

It was called the Fabian Society progressive movement, a socialist minded group of individuals. Bernard Shaw being one of them shortly after 1884.

Its main purpose was to secretly form a New World government. To form or create just treatment for the society of British workers, became one of their goals. This would then become the beginning of England's welfare state.

Their workers were to have, cheap council housing, free dental care, free medicine and spectacles. Also, this would be given to all the workers from their colonies which were many, like Singapore and Malaya. There also would be generous unemployment benefits.

This was offered as a well-planned attraction, to having any other forms of governments. It was not realized until the 1970's that this program put forth by the progressive Fabian Society was greatly inept.

That it was the beginning of huge problems, and that it contributed wholly to the decline of the British economy.

There was a slow transfer to socialism, and it was the beginning of the people to rely on government for the general needs of the people, thereby forcing the government to tax the wealthy to satisfy the needs of the poor.

As this trend continued to grow, the appearance of fairness to the people would also grow, giving socialism a foothold in the governing body of a nation.

How this takes place is that an organization must be formed to fight for the rights of the general public. A farce in reality, but very effective in winning over the will of the people, especially in a society where voting on issues is the policy of the land. The Fabian society have now used the government to advance their socialist ways. They start to take control in very secretive ways.

The organizations they form give the appearance that they fought and won for the people, because of the many benefits that they will receive, when it reality, is was made possible by taxing the people.

The Fabian society was named in honor of the Roman general, Fabians Maximus, who was given a nickname "Cunctator" which means delayer. His strategy was to harass the enemy, rather than to have a head on battle. These tactics were used very successfully against the Carthaginian Army that fought under the renowned general Hannibal.

The Fabian society will slowly and methodically infiltrate into the fabric of a foreign government, that they want to change into a socialist nation.

They will form organizations like the ACLU, have their lawyers find loopholes in the laws that govern a nation, then slowly over time, alter them to conform to their ideology.

They will do that covertly, with any means available to them, having no problem to deceive, or even murder. They will do whatever it takes to disrupt and demoralize a nation, in order to achieve their goals, in the most secretive ways. To them, it is politically correct to do so, to complete their mission of creating a Socialist Society.

They realize that it is a slow march to world dominance. They have been aggressively applying their efforts on the United States in many ways for most of the last hundred years. The socialist has gained positions in our senate, our congress, now with this present administration, are also in the president's cabinet.

I believe that the strength of our Constitution, our Bill of Rights and our will to be a free nation has prevailed so far. However, they, the Fabian Society's Progressive Movement, have never stopped pursuing their goals. This once great nation has become extremely unstable. This nation cannot tolerate another four years of liberalism.

Our problem is, that we don't have a goal, we haven't realized we need a goal. There are few in this country that even know that the Fabian Society even exist. Let us not be fooled - they do exist.

They are the most dangerous enemy of the American people. They have already inserted themselves and have gained a strong influence into our governing body. Done so because they have gained the support of their pawns, that are their loyal Democratic party.

The Fabian Society have been bringing harm to our shores for the last hundred years. This movement is real and is a serious threat to the citizens of our free nation.

After all the years of them wanting to destroy our governing body and replace it with their ideas, they have slowly and successfully been doing this. Few in this country recognize what has been taking place right before their eyes.

Over the years through their pawns in the Democratic party and the liberal media, which they were instrumental in creating, was their plan to achieve their goal of World dominance.

They have successfully used our government to form many Liberal organizations paid for with our taxes, that they used very efficiently against our Government, State by State.

They, I believe, have heavily invested, through lobbyist's, in the EPA (Environmental Protection Agency), Planned Parenthood, Global warming, the ACLU (American Civil Liberties Union) and the C.P.C. (Congressional Progressive Caucus), to name a few, all of which have slowed down our economy, with federal rules and regulations, that has forced many of our businesses to move to other countries.

To name some of them, Mexico and especially China and India, have profited greatly because of this. They have taken over most of our manufacturing and technical jobs that had been driving a large portion of our economy. Close to seventy-five percent of all technical jobs have also been lost to other countries. The truth of this is realized in the true number of unemployed here in America.

I believe that it was around the year 1939, approximately 75 years ago, when they successfully penetrated our school system and started to make changes in the schools of this nation. They have named this method of teaching, the progressive system of education.

After a few years of studying the results of this new approach to teaching, it became evident that American history would be changed and discredited in every way possible. It also became evident that future generations of students would learn very little of how our laws are processed or how our government functions.

They would also gain control over and strongly influence our children's minds, leading them down a path to socialism. They have been doing this now, year after year, since 1939, enforcing the liberal agenda into the young minds of America's children all across our land.

They have also been touting the democratic party as the party to trust and believe in. This has been happening now for 75 years and no one ever questions why.

Have we become unaware that more than 75% of

teachers in our schools are liberal and in our colleges the percentage is even higher. When are we going to fight to take back our schools?

Our American hero's and great presidents of our past will never be taught about, or are even mentioned in our schools. History books will change, be rewritten to glorify the progressive movement happening in our country, in the most subliminal ways.

Today, when questioned by some of our news media on the streets of our cities, many college students do not know who our first president was, and are not even sure who our vice president might be at the present time. College students do not know who Columbus was, and many cannot name the year America was discovered.

Our Public School system is floored and very expensive to run. In many schools throughout our country, our children are not receiving an education at all. They are just being taught a liberal agenda. This is exactly what the progressives wanted, and it is happening today, in our schools throughout America.

It is only in the private and Catholic schools that this may not be taking place. This is one of the reasons why the liberal Democrats fight so hard not to have school vouchers. It apparently is very important to the progressive movement, not to lose revenue to private schools.

Also, it is just as important to have a larger student body, to keep student numbers at a minimum or none at all in private schools. This gives the unions more money and power to achieve their goals.

Besides, the more children that they have in the public school systems, the odds become greater to be able to mold students into becoming liberal voting democrats of the future.

Students going to private or parochial schools may grow up and become a resistance to their movement, which would hinder their plans of socializing this nation. But some Liberal teachers in the sixties have managed to penetrate Catholic high schools also.

It has been approximately 85 or 90 years ago since they have successfully implemented this Fabian society's progressive movement in America. They may with this next presidential election be ready to make their move to take control of this country. Another liberal administration might give them fuel needed to change our nation into a socialist society.

They have successfully planted 70 or more socialists into our Congress that hold congressional seats. They were very successful in having voted in

President Obama twice, a socialist president who has installed as his cabinet, known communist members.

The many organizations' that were cleverly structured, have been doing their dirty work practically for the last 90 years or more, and have continued to grow stronger over the many years of their existence. All of these organizations were started and remain funded with our tax dollars.

Therefore, due to the many years that they have had to sharpen their skills, they have also been able to earn revenue from their activities, and this has rendered them overwhelmingly powerful.

One would only have to research the department and size of these many monstrous organization's and their effort's made, that the Fabian Society have used, to install this progressive movement and is actively taking place now, in our country.

Try to understand the extreme danger we are facing. They have their forearm against the throat of America with a dagger poised to penetrate the heart of our nation, and this could be done at a moment's notice. It's hard to understand why the Democratic pawns of this movement still cannot realize the grave danger this nation is facing.

The Liberal Democrats just don't get it. They,

along with the rest of us, will suffer the consequences of the United States becoming a socialist nation. They don't seem to realize what is taking place in our country, and that is very worrisome.

They probably have no idea or even know of the Fabian Society, nor do they realize how the progressives are tied to the Fabian Society movement in our country. Few people do.

It is an evil organization, and to be successful in achieving their goal, their best weapon is the skill that they have developed in the secretive ways they go about their business.

They know the people whose government they seek to covert to socialism. These socialists have been using the democrats to help them in their endeavor.

However, I believe these democrats would turn against them at a moment's notice if they found out what they are really about.

I believe that democrats have been used, that they have been from the day they entered school, and have been programmed by the progressives to vote for liberal causes.

The Fabian society needs to have one more victory at the presidency to continue their progressive ways.

We must stop this from happening. With a strong conservative in the white house, we could stop them from advancing further.

To defeat them we must first understand who our enemies are. Our Constitution and our Bill of Rights has been standing strong in-spite of the aggression from the left proving how marvelous a document it is, and that our forefathers gave to us over 240 years ago.

However, we must take our country back and restore it to what it was before the progressive's started to make changes in our government and in our schools. Changes that have stymied our progress starting some ninety years ago. It will take a strong President to make our country great again.

The Fabian Society have developed so many organizations in the United States, and that is working against us. It has bolstered their movement, and it may be too great a struggle to overcome.

Our great Republic is at a critical point in history. Our next presidential election can be a turning point in the lives of all American's. We have come to a fork in the road of the lives of all American's, both present and future, and both Democratic or Republican alike.

Our forefathers, have given us a path that we may walk, and that will guide us and remain with us for the rest of our lives. They have brought us this far and have given us true freedom, that has made our nation the envy of the oppressed throughout the world.

We are at a point where firm decisions must be made. For a very long time now, the progressive movement have secretively been fighting against the conservative right. If the right loses this struggle, there will be no going back to the free nation that we once were.

This road that we are destined to walk, will lead this nation to the left or to the right of history. The Fabian Progressive's successfully convinced a huge number of voters in United States to walk the left side of the road. I honestly don't know if the people now walking this road on the left, really know much about the path they have chosen.

The builders of this road on the left do know. They have carefully laid out a path for the Liberal Democrats to follow, with the support they receive from school unions, and other organizations on the left like the ACLU, EPA, Planned Parenthood, Global Warming and so many more.

They have developed many skills that they used convincingly over the years, of having extreme power because of the wealth of these organizations. This enabled them to gain influence, through lobbying from the left, to vote favorably for causes that benefit Fabian Society movements.

Donations from school unions, that have become extremely wealthy, has helped these unions develop strong relationships with the democratic branches of our Senate and Congress. This marriage of unions with the democratic branches of government, has become a normal occurrence.

The influence that School unions have over our Board of Education has enabled them to push our students to the liberal left. This has been going on for seventy-five years or more, unchecked and worse, unchallenged by anyone.

Our public schools and colleges have become a propaganda mechanism for the Fabian society's progressive movement and successfully so. This is not what our forefathers had planned for our nation.

For any situation that may arise, that they fear would get in the way of their ultimate plan - to socialize America - a program would be made to counter the opposition immediately.

The ACLU, with the two hundred plus lawyers at their disposal, could place twenty attorneys or more if necessary, to bring satisfying results in their favor, often resulting in our taxes paying for the program.

This has resulted in a multitude of leftist organizations developing here in our governments across this country.

This has been sneakily taking place, quietly for over ninety to a hundred years. It has finally brought this nation to a fork in the road. With a path on the left that is strong and powerful in their quest to world dominance which was started by the Fabian Society over a 130 years ago till now.

The reality of them, in control of this world, I don't think will ever happen, but I do believe that if the Fabian Society is not stopped, it could continue to destroy our nation in the process. However, making us become a socialist country, could happen.

The opportunity can become ours, to reverse their progress, and expose them for what they truly are all about. The United States, while saving our country, in the process, we would be exposing them to the world.

Then nations under their control, as is Great Britain and the whole of Europe, might follow our example and take back control from the Fabian's Society also.

The progressive movement has not done a single thing to help our nation. So what right do they have, to take charge of what the brave fighting men and women of this land died for. Men and women that bravely died fighting to preserve our freedom.

This divide, which started here in the United States about 90 years ago, with the progressive's true motive, I firmly believe has yet to be fully understood. Neither the republicans or the Democrats, really are aware of this movement which will affect the lives of all free people here and throughout the world. The big advantage that they have, has been their secretiveness.

The Fabian Socialist have managed over many long years to hide behind the cover of a progressive label. They managed successfully to keep hidden the war that Americans were engaged in, to remove from our history the greatness of a nation that our forefathers had given us.

It has become difficult to find a book in the schools of America that will tell the truth about the early history of this great nation. Why haven't historians or our governing body questioned or investigated this? Is there no way of controlling this liberal movement?

We the people of these United States of America, as plagued as we are by this movement, have so far survived, by the strength of the written words giving to us by our forefathers. They have kept the good people of this nation on the right side of the road.

Can we imagine? The Constitution, that the framers of this great nation gave to us, a four-page document of 4200 words, written on 4 pieces of parchment, with the fifth piece of parchment being a letter of transmittal, and the 6th piece of parchment being the writings of the Bill of Rights, has proven to be more powerful than the Fabian's Society efforts of the last 90 years or more.

Our Constitution, our Bill of Rights, having been challenged so many times by the left, still stands alone, as the most powerful doctrine ever written. It has created for the people of this nation, a strong and powerful beginning, that can only lead, for the first time in the existence of modern man, a nation that is truly free.

We cannot become a socialist America. We cannot, we must not, let this happen to us. Both Hillary and Obama have claimed to be progressive Democrat's and they say it proudly. Is this what we want running our country?

How can we, our American Government, or the citizens of any civilized nation not see the evil battle that is taking place in America? What is happening to our nation and the effect it would have worldwide should we fail?

We must make all of the people realize and believe the truth of what is taking place here. This Fabian Society has been developing programs that are designed to take down our country. They are always there ready to protest to make changes to benefit their idea of transforming this country over to socialism.

They have hundreds of thousands of men and women working for them, with a large army of lawyer's. All are citizens of this country. All mostly paid for with our taxes, are there to counter our Constitution and our Bill of Rights. Their intense effort to do so, has slowly taken effect.

They are the enemy of ALL the American people, Liberal Democrats and Republicans alike. They have been at war with America for the last 90 years. We have to understand that this is a huge army of our own citizens that they are using to defeat us. This is no different than armed combat.

We have been invaded over 90 years ago and their fight will not be over until they have complete control of our government.

It is no different than having a cancer invade your body and slowly eat at the very substance of every organ in your being until you cannot function any longer.

Like a cancer, the Fabian progressives' have America at that point, at the brink of collapsing very soon if we continue to not recognize our enemy.

I don't think we have yet, but they will have us on our knees, they will have won their War. They will have accomplished what they started 90 years ago, without firing a single shot, without most of the people of this country even knowing that we were at war with this cancer eating relentlessly at the foundation of our great nation.

They have successfully, with their sneaky approach, been able to keep most of America in the dark all of these years.

If the ruling body of our government and the people of this country can be convinced of the danger this nation is facing, then and only then, can survival still be had and we can win this war, but only if we wake up! We have to wake up, know that we are in a very serious war, and we must treat this as a war. We must recognize our enemy and fight to defeat them soundly, and we can.

They have already taken control of Great Britain, the place where the Fabian Society was born. Also, they have successfully involved themselves into all the countries of Europe. There is more to be said about how their influence has socialized England and all of the nations of Europe.

They are now involved in every move that Great Britain and the countries of Europe make. No decisions involving serious negotiations in this area of the globe can now, by their laws, be made in the countries of Europe and those of Great Britain, without the presence of the Fabian Society. This organization, the Fabian Society, has been relentless in the pursuant of their goals.

All of these left leaning organizations, every one of them, have got to be dismantled. We, must understand, they were all formed and designed as weapons to defeat this nation. Therefore, we, Americans, to protect our nation from defeat, have every right to destroy them.

They declared this war. So we have every right to use any means possible to become victorious in this battle for survival, to return to what our forefathers laid out for us. To be a free nation under god with justice and liberty for all.

America needs the help of every person in this country both men and women, Democrat and Republican alike, to join in this battle. Listen up America - This is a WAR that we are in and it must be fought as a WAR. We either pull together and fight, OR continue to let our enemy keep us divided as they have been doing for the past 90 years.

Unless the people of this nation believe that there is a battle to be fought, that there is an evil enemy living in our house, we will all be destined to fail.

My prayers are with the people of our great nation. Please, let's not let this nation fail. Research what I have been saying, it is all there for you to see, if you would take the time to look it up.

Never before in our history has there been so defined a choice to be made to save this nation. The choices made on election day, may be the reality of the warning given to us by Benjamin Franklin so many years ago, when he said: "*A Republic Madam if you can keep it*".

I cannot understand where the liberals think they will be if the United States loses its freedom? If this nation comes under the control of a socialist government, the liberal's will suffer the same faith that all of America will face under these circumstances.

I feel strongly that the progressives are not pleased with the selection of the Democratic candidates that are campaigning to be the next democratic president. The Republican candidates will produce a winner against what the Democrats are offering to be the nominee for their party.

The Progressive Movement cannot let this happen. It would be a major setback to their cause, if a Republican president takes control of the White House, while the Republicans already have a majority in both houses.

The Fabian's have been working on taking control of the United States, very successfully, for about a Hundred years. If we added all the monies, from every Organization they have either installed and/or owned, and these monies are made available to them, it would amount to Hundreds of Billions of dollars.

Also, consider the amount of men and women working for the ACLU, EPA, FEA, NEA and the C.P.C., to mention a few, that are well organized and are working on their behalf.

Try to imagine the power of their work force, that they have at their disposal. The ACLU has a working staff of more than 500,000, including a minimum of two hundred lawyers.

The strength of the NEA is overwhelming - they have the force of 2.3 million school teachers and approximately 1 million workers, as bus drivers, custodians and food servers. A work force of NEA workers so large that it is more than half of the union members working for local governments. It is believed to be, the largest unionized portion of the United States economy.

It can be considered an Army of Democrats that have been fighting for Liberal or Socialist causes for many decades. They have become a fighting force of at least 4 million men and women strong.

This is a huge advantage over Conservatives, that so many on the right do not even realize there is a battle going on. It has been going on! If something can't be seen, that does not mean it is non existing.

Most of the Conservative interest has been the preservation of our Constitution and our Bill of Rights. These were written to ensure that our freedom remains guarded, and to protect what the brave men and women of our past and the present, have died fighting for.

The vast majority of the US citizens, have never heard of the Fabian Society because they are so secretive. They have been hiding behind the progressive movement as Liberal Democrat's, the pawns of the Democratic Party.

I have asked many people over the years and, even more so, in the last few weeks, if they have ever heard of this organization, called "The Fabian

Society", progressive movement. Their answer was no. They do not even seem to care - this is where the danger lies. I would want to know who our enemies are, where they are from and what their intentions are.

Some have heard of progressives, and believe it is exactly what the word progress suggests. That it is an advanced way of viewing the political structure of this nation. It is exactly what the left would want the public to think, perfect for their camouflage.

Knowing the evilness of their plans for the American people is sickening. How terrible is the idea of stealing freedom that people have, and replacing it with a dictatorial form of government? Let us not fool ourselves, this is exactly what their plan is.

The evil that the Fabian Society really represents, remains hidden, the evil truth of their plan that has been hidden from so many for so long, may soon be realized. It is frightening to accept, that America will become a socialist nation. I pray that I am wrong. But it can happen if we don't start to recognize our adversaries.

What is happening within our government, with these vast amounts of liberal associations has placed us on the brink of we the people of These United Stated in losing their freedom.

They are invisible to most, but are there, battling hard to destroy us.

This nation, the United States of America, as a very young nation had achieved greatness. It had proven that free people will prosper, without the restrictions of big Dictatorial types of government.

It had given hope to the oppressed people of this world, that if their Government would learn from America to set their people free, that the will of free people naturally excels and would be a lesson well learned for the oppressors of humans on this Earth.

America has not reached its full potential. The promise of this nation's greatness has not yet been realized. After the first world war, America was at the threshold of advancing to a style of living with true prosperity for its people.

The capacity of people in a free nation to excel was there. We grew past the restrictions placed on people by overpowering governments. It just did not exist in America.

This expression of freedom that was being sort could not be accomplished under any other form of government on this planet, except ours, the United

States of America. The legacy of our Constitution and of our Bill of Rights has come to be a guarantee to this end.

We the people of this great nation must take stock of who we are and where we stand in this world as of today. We as a nation under this present administration is starting to crumble.

As it stands now, in our president's cabinet, is the making of a socialistic structure. A cabinet of his design can only mean that our president has no desire to lead this nation, in a manner that would strengthen our Republic. It tells us that he is preparing a socialistic agenda for the American people.

If another socialist man or women is voted in as president, we have then as a nation, in my opinion, started to see the birth of socialism in America, slowly taking over our nation.

With a phone and a pen, once again, laws will be changed to alter our Constitution. New laws will be made to silence our Senate and congress, rendering them to become, totally insignificant bodies in our law making process.

If this trend to become a socialistic nation continues, the hope of the oppressed people of this world to seek a place to settle and truly be free will have vanished. True freedom for the people of this world will never be realized ever again.

What is happening now, is that the United States is being attacked in the most sinister way imaginable, by an enemy that knows how to hide behind and also use, the laws of the nation they are attacking, to advance their causes.

We in America have unknowingly been plagued for most of the last hundred years, by a man-made cancer that was designed to cowardly undermine this nation.

It would make more sense to have a world where people can live independent lives, free of the fear which comes with being oppressed, than to have to live under the rule of what the Fabian Society and our president wants for us in America, and eventually the rest of the world.

We need a very strong conservative candidate to be up for president in this coming election. We need to convince the men and women of this nation that, regardless of party, it has become extremely important that the voting public realize that party affiliation cannot be a deciding factor in this particular presidential race.

We as a free nation, to remain as a free nation, must

not let a candidate, selected by the progressive movement, become our next President, as was the case in our last two elections. For we are not running Republican against Democrat, we are not even voting to create a stronger party.

We are voting to save a nation, our nation, that we fought so hard for in our past. A nation that has shown the ordinary people of this world, that the strength of a nation is in their people, not the government. In reality, we are voting for our freedom to remain intact.

Know that we also, are voting for our lives. It is NOW, one of those rare times in our history, that we must unify once more. It is time to fight back against those that seek to take away our freedom. The time has come for us to recognize who our enemies really are.

Although we have a fighting force in physical combat, half a world away, our most dangerous enemy is here at our front door. They have been there for 90 years or more.

Imagine, they have been silently attacking us constantly over so long a period of time and 99% of our government, or the American people, know little or nothing about them.

Americans must come together now, for our very

existence as a nation, is in jeopardy. I cannot impress you enough, of the importance of this next election, the danger we face can be proven, if you would take the time to research the Fabian Society.

What I am telling you, is true, the enemy I speak of, is real, the danger we are in, is eminent. This cancer that is eating at the guts of our country must be stopped.

Both parties must stand together as one. Let's not be fooled, if a new face emerges as a Democrat, or under any other party, it should raise a red flag.

We must no longer kid ourselves, we will need the strength of the Democratic vote to show solidarity to this evil progressive movement, which has controlled and unfairly been using the democrats as a front, for so many years.

I am guessing that the progressives will find a younger, more vibrant person, that will be selected and inserted into the race for president. If Hillary or Bernie Sanders, if one of them, does not come up strong, if they appear as though they cannot win, or any other candidate that is seeking to be nominated on the Democratic side, appears weak and beatable, a candidate will emerge to the liken of the progressive movement, and may very well be voted in and nominated to run on the Democratic ticket to become our next President.

They, with the billions of dollars available to them from socialistic union's, especially school unions and the strength of their propaganda machines, in the liberal media and in Hollywood, along with their skills in modifying the voting machines, a new candidate could be presented by the democratic establishment, to run against the republican nominee.

I imagine that they would have created a figurehead to take the place of Obama and if this happens and he or she becomes president, then, it will be another Obama in our White House. It then will become only a matter of time, for this nation to be under socialist rule.

We know that, in America, is about the only place in this world, where people are truly free. Only Israel comes close to the degree of freedom that we Americans have enjoyed since our birth and the birth of this nation.

Our present government seems to be on a campaign to take our freedom away from us, destroy our United States, resulting in the definite loss of our freedom.

Under this administration our power has weakened drastically, we are losing respect among our allies and enemies alike. He has weakened our military by under-funding it. Why? Does he believe, that we are not in a war. Our President Obama cannot say the word Jihad. What is he afraid of?

President Obama, as Senator Obama, complained about the national debt of Ten Trillion Dollars that only part of which, was generated under the watch of President Bush.

The liberal press, I believe, under the guidance of the progressive movement, criticized the Bush administration and the republican party endlessly, as they would do with any other issue that they could find, to harass and intimidate the Republicans.

However, President Obama's national debt is now more than Eighteen Trillion Dollars, almost doubled what it was under President Bush, in only a little over six years and still rising. Also, on Obama's watch, Iran may be on its way to having nuclear weapons.

An agreement made with Iran by Secretary of State, Kerry, and agreed to by President Obama, has a strong chance of passing through the Senate, because the Senate liberal democrats will always stay in lockstep with their leader, right or wrong. It has little regard for what is good for our allies or our country or even the safety of the American people.

They over the years have learned to do as they are

told by the leftist members of their party, regardless of the consequences. On this issue they could not be more mistaken. Can this be about talking points once more?

They have the Iranian leader saying "Down with America", as Kerry is sitting down with Iranian negotiators. With all the talking being done, only indicates that Iran will have a bomb in less than ten years. So will Obama be saying that Bin Laden is dead, Al Qaeda is on the run and we stopped Iran's Nuclear program?

This recent agreement, that has placed our faithful ally, Israel, in great danger of being attacked, does not weigh heavy on the minds of the democrats. Because of the democrats' strong alliance with the Obama administration, they seem not to care if nuclear bombs are dropped on the Jewish state of Israel, or that our national security is being jeopardized by this poorly written agreement.

What seems to be important to the Liberal Democrat's, is that they stay in support, unconditionally, with president Obama and the progressive movement which I believe, has been planted in our White House.

Listen, yes, the silence from the liberal democrats and the left news media remains deafening, as always. What will it take to make them realize that there is a movement in place to take over this nation, to become part of a World Order, that the enemy which is presently at our doorstep has made huge gains, while this present administration has been in our White House.

Does anyone on the liberal left realize that they are the pawns of this progressive movement? That they are being used by this movement?

Take the time to look them up, realize what is in store for you if your freedom is lost and Socialism becomes the law of this land.

This will still be the land that Democrats and their families will also have to live in and will also feel the oppression that Socialism brings.

You won't have to concern yourself about party affiliation, you will be told that you love being a Socialist. Don't deny the love for Socialism that you have, or you may ponder how you feel about that, while in jail for the next ten years or more.

Ask the citizens of China, Russia or Cuba about their lives under socialist rule. I have! While talking with a few that were vacationing in this country, I expressed a few views that I have of this administration.

They cringed in fear, even thousands of miles away

from their native land. I could see it in their eyes the pain and fear they have and also in their expressions, that worrisome look, that somebody could be watching them.

All they would say to me was, that how I expressed myself would never be tolerated in their country. That even members of their family may tell the authorities on them.

It was a sad note in my mind, I thought, may God bless America how wonderful it is to have the freedom that we have here in this country of ours.

Is this the way the people of America want to live in constant fear of government? Living with members of your own family that will spy on you. Imagine, who can you trust in a Socialist society, if not even your own family?

Our enemy knows that what they have in store for us, will be the end of our freedom. They will put us under a new set of laws that would make the people of this nation, silent slaves under their control. The voice of the people will never be heard again. Nothing on television, or written in newspapers will be believable. All you see or read about will be under the control of the government.

When America is transformed into a socialist Government. It will not take them very long to remove all of our inalienable rights given to us, the American people by our forefathers.

It was important for them to be very secretive, because they know how evil this plan against us is. Why would anyone want to give up so precious a gift that our forefathers gave to America and to its citizens.

If the truth is told to the American people, that this real plan is to socialize America, I believe that Democrat's also would reject the idea of socialism for our people.

What gall does it take? How can anyone force people to believe this is good for them? To bring socialism to a nation of 321 million people, change the people's lives completely around. All their gains they have made in their lifetime of work, can be taken away from them with the stroke of a pen.

Our president knows there is no gain to the general public, under the rule of socialism. Where are the moderate Democrat's to stand against this man, that has been manipulating the American people with lies, since 2008 when he first was elected?

Do we really know if our president is a true Democrat, or is he a socialist like Bernie Sanders? And who can believe Hillary Clinton?

Obama, our President, visited Cuba. I believe he is the first American president to do so since Cuba was declared a Communist nation. Will Raul or Fidel Castro become more civil with their people?

Will a deal be made to set the Cuban citizens free of socialist reform that they were forced to live under for so many years?

Did President Obama seek to convince Cuban leadership to change to a Republic, or become a more Democratic society? Remove the hardship of socialism that breathes fear into the hearts and minds of its people?

What did Obama ask for, in exchange for a diplomatic relationship, that can only benefit the Cuban government and not that of their people.

Why wouldn't the United States make some demands of Cuba in exchange for this diplomatic deal, or is there something else happening here, that is not being told?

The progressives can never tell you the truth about their real goals, because the average liberal person on the left only believe what they are told to believe to be the truth. They, I believe, don't know what the truth really is, what the progressive movement tells them is true, is what they blindly adhere to.

Their real ambition of world dominance is kept secret from the public, they will never admit that is what their goal really is.

But if you reference the internet, the information about the progressive Fabian Society is available for anyone to read. This is not only happening here in the United States. The Fabian Society has been very active and successful in England and all of Europe.

Although slow moving, it is methodologically taking its effect here in America. They are experts at propaganda and especially good at telling lies.

Listen to the lies about Benghazi, a little less than two months before Obama's presidential election.

Hillary still cannot own up to what the truth is. It would only work against her plans of becoming our next president. So she will continue to lie to the American people.

His Health Care Plan, was to be the best plan ever for the American people. Well is it? I sometimes believe we will never be able to stop their progress.

We can, if the moderate democrats will open their eyes to the truth and start living up to our Constitution, and fight for what is good for our country for a change. Join us in electing a man that will fight to make America great again.

Unless we can get the moderate and liberal democrats to see and understand how they are being used by the Fabian society's movement for so long, over the many years of their existence, they may very well succeed to change this country into a socialist nation.

Why any president would want America to become a socialist nation is for personal gain only. Not for the people he took an oath to protect.

It will be a sad happening to the oppressed people of this world. All who have had dreams of living in a free society, to legally becoming citizens of this great nation, or to establish the American way in their country. It will become just a dream and nothing more. There never again, will be a place to ever escape to, with a dream to become free and to prosper. How shameful will that be?

All factors of this taking place in America is in plain view, if the public would just open their eyes, understand what is taking place in this country for so many years. Ask. Just ask why? Ask why did George Soros donate millions of dollars to rioters? It is on record that he gave Thirty-Three Million Dollars to the rioters in Ferguson.

What business was it of his, to donate that much money or any money at all. That aided and abetted the crimes of the rioters. Has there been any outcry at all from the liberal media, to call out George Soros for a crime he may have committed.

Is this a paid organized force to disrupt and dismantle that local governments in the United states? Is this a move to social reform? Why George? Are you also a progressive?

Ask why the police forces in this country are being attacked? Is this also part of the Fabian movement, to silence and disrupt authority? Is Mr. Soros part of this progressive movement to dismantle this free nation?

I often wonder why people of this nation and of this world, don't ask, why! Hollywood is so liberal? Why! Our teachers, especially in our colleges, are so liberal?

Why! Our news media and our newspapers, are so liberal! All this liberal control did not just happen on its own. All of this was strategically planned and happened over many decades by the socialist progressive Fabian organization, who are striving to eventually create and put in place a new world order.

The men and women that first organized the Fabian

Society's progressive idea, have long ago passed on. But the goals that they presented and put into action in 1884 are very much alive to this day.

This movement continues to grow. The men and women that are active in this progressive movement, the progressive Fabian Society, have long ago realized that America's republic must fall, so that socialism or the Progressive movement can expand.

I imagine they believe, that many others nations, allied to America will also fail and can easily be controlled in the demise or the destruction of the United States.

A weak economy can destroy a nation from within. Is this what is happening to our country, is a movement taking place with a phone and pen? Is there a movement, a growing force ready to overcome us?

Just stop to think. Ask why would George Soros back rioters and pay them thirty-three million dollars to create the havoc they did?

Why is there so little news about this? Rioters that were bused in to burn and destroy businesses in Ferguson. And the Liberal News media has nothing to say.

Shouldn't Mr. Soros be held accountable for the many cars and businesses that were destroyed? Who are these looters that were bused in? How many are there, under the control of George Soros? Are they the same men and women that occupy Wall Street? Are they all on George Soros payroll? Is George Soros declaring war on America?

I cannot see any reason why a man like George with the billions of dollars at his disposal would not embrace our Constitution and back this great nation. What can be gained by supporting looters.

Is the silence of the press an indication that the progressive movement gained enough strength, that they became emboldened in their quest to world dominance? Does their boldness tell us that they feel that the United States is ready to fold?

I feel strongly that most liberals either have no idea, or that they are well informed about the Democratic party's alliance with the progressive movement in this country. Or are they aware that there is a plan that will transform this nation over to socialism. That it is they, who are contributing to the demise of this great nation.

Most who graduate from our colleges, who find themselves hating this country, have blindly been moved to the left and have been firmly programmed to become the future pawns for this progressive movement.

The professors in our educational system, have cleverly learned how to select the weaker minded students into believing the liberal viewpoints. They trust and blindly fight for all the programs that are said to be politically correct.

And in most cases these programs that are formed and organized by the left, eventually are found to be corrupt and extremely expensive to operate, regardless of whatever their expense becomes. Our tax dollars will be there to take care of them.

One recent example is Planned Parenthood which has been making millions of dollars from selling baby body parts. The person in charge is receiving a salary which exceeds $500,000 dollars a year. Still, this organization receives millions from the United States government.

The liberal Democrats cannot see a reason to stop funding this program with our tax dollars. The Democrats claim they are the only party that is looking out for us.

This plays well with the progressive movement. Their goal is to bankrupt this nation as our present progressive's leaders are doing, because they are aware that if you want to capture a nation, destroy their economy.

Obama and his spending, plays well for the Fabian Society progressive movement. Obama is doing exactly as the progressives want. He has rapidly been eating away at our economy.

He is not a foolish man. His giveaway programs have effectively been increasing the size of government. This is exactly what he wants to happen. It all plays well to weaken our country, America, as is his goal.

I believe that if the democratic men and women of this country read about men like Obama and his political affiliation with socialism, also read and understand what the Fabian Society progressive movement is really about, they would not have nominated him for president, they would change their minds about who to listen to and to believe.

Some would stop being the pawns for this Fabian Society's progressive organization.

The progressive Fabian society movement was established approximately 130 years ago. Their goal was to dominate the world and create a new world order. Their method, I believe, is to infiltrate into the government of a nation and alter their laws to favor their progressive ideology.

They accomplish this by forming organizations, that they manage to convince the government, that they would be a benefit to the American people.

Also, they will lobby politicians that they gave large donations to, helping them to get elected, knowing they will be useful in passing laws to benefit their activities.

We must realize that many of the organization's formed by the progressives were put in place probably, a little less than a hundred years ago. Some may have had names changes, but their purpose remains the same under the different names of what they are today.

As was, Planned Parenthood. It was started in 1916, by a women named Mary Ware Dennet. She, having named it, the national Birth Control League.

It was taken over by an activist woman named Margaret Sanger, she changed the name to, American Birth Control League.

In years following, the center changed its name once again to become Planned Parenthood Federation of America, Inc.

The ACLU was also formed in the early nineteen hundredths. So were many other organizations and school unions. None of these organization just happened coincidentally. Most were formed purposely to assist the efforts of the progressive movement.

This had to be accomplished in secretive ways. It must have been realized by the progressives, that if they are not seen as connected to the Fabian society's movement, that they would then be able to do their dirty work unrestrained.

This approach would not be necessary if their plans for the people of this land was honest and good for the people. But they know that their evil must be hidden in order to be effective in achieving their goal of world dominance.

I imagine that they believed that the United States would have to become a socialized nation. To accomplish this, it would be made easy, if they aligned themselves to a political party.

I feel strongly that when they decided, about 95 years ago, to move in on the United States, they believed at that time, that the Democratic party was a much stronger organization than the Republican party. It would be wiser to control the more dominant of the two parties, to achieve their goal, which in their minds, were the Democrats.

They, very successfully to this day, have made deep

inroads into the Democratic Party. So much so, that it has become somewhat difficult to tell if they are Democrats or Socialists when they express their political views.

Imagine this, Chris Matthews, a liberal newsman on MSNBC News, asked Debby Wassermann Schultz, a strong advocate for the Democrats, if she could explain the difference between a socialist or a Democrat. She could not.

But to her defense, nobody can. Nobody can because there is no difference. Nobody can, because the Democratic party has been completely transformed to now being, a Socialist leftist organization.

Nobody can, because the Democrats have lost their direction. They have become Pawns for the Socialist Progressive movement taking place in America.

When will they open their eyes and realize what they have become? Or do the democrats really want to see this country become Socialized?

If these events of change to our government, were ever to take place, either party could have been chosen to work for their causes. Neither party will mean anything at all to the Fabian society, because they brought about liberalism only as a way to ease their socialist ideology onto the public.

Once they are in charge, both parties will be dismantled. The liberals would have served their purpose. They, and all people of this country, will be forced into becoming citizens of one Socialist party.

The voices that were free to express their viewpoints will be silenced. No one, except a chosen few, will have a voice in the behavior of a socialist governing body, as is the case in all communist, dictatorial or socialist operating governments.

They will do anything necessary or use anyone they can by any and all means possible, to achieve their goal. This could become the faith of our nation. We must take control of our country and get back to being the Republic we once were.

They also needed a strong propaganda vehicle. The movie industry was in it's infancy after the first World War. What better time was there to start, what became their strong influence over Hollywood, with the launching of their propaganda machine?

It was also a good time for them to start incorporating the Democratic party as their vehicle to launch their plans of guiding this America into becoming a socialist nation.

We can see evidence of this happening back as far as the 1920's in silent movies with Charlie Chaplin, marching in step, in a union parade, and carrying a red flag displaying a hammer and cycle.

Then there was Errol Flynn as Robin Hood. Remember that great movie? I believe it was released in 1938 and was all about robbing from the rich and giving to the poor.

Earlier in the 1930's with Spenser Tracy, they would have an actor in the movie do something foolish and jokingly, Tracy would then say, "he must be a Republican." These subliminal messages can be seen and heard, in many old movies, many times over.

I personally believe, that there are several reasons why plans that the progressive movement has of, "A One world government," would be impossible for them to implement. I will mention a few. Just the World's population of 7.3 Billion at the present time and growing, is too overwhelming.

Their plan to alter the laws of governments and their method of doing it, has them moving at a snail's pace. While the population of the world continues its rapid growth, making it impossible for them to keep pace with it. This alone may be difficult to overcome for their plan to work. Also, the religion of some of the middle east countries, I believe, would be extremely difficult to overcome.

But this doesn't mean that the methods that they have deployed have not done considerable damage to the stability and the well-being of people of various nations. England and all of Europe are suffering as the result of the progressives' involvement in their governments.

America being one nation, that has suffered gravely, for now approaching a 100 years, as a result of the many organizations that the progressive movement has developed and installed into the structure of our government, to destroy our economy.

They also, to a degree, have very successfully eroded the foundation of our Constitution and our Bill of Rights to do so. They have tried to demoralized the very image of what our flag stands for.

Rioters burning and trampling our flag, right here in the streets of America, is considered to be politically correct by the left. Therefore, it is alright, for the many who oppose this action, to stand by and capitulate to the few.

These demonstrations, which pierce the hearts of

the majority of Americans, continue to go unchallenged by our government and the liberal press. It leaves the impression that the American people are doing the demonstrating, when they are not.

It is the marauders that are paid to panic the people, to make the world believe that our country is in disarray. That the people living here are unhappy and dissatisfied with our government. All part of the way the progressive operates to bring down a nation. Sadly, I must admit that their plans of demonstrating the nasty way that they have, does work.

Huge salaries are paid to the members of their work force, also to the many organizations, most of which is paid for with our taxes. It may be part of the reason why we now have an $18 plus trillion-dollar debt. If we, as a nation, cannot see what is happening with the progressive movement, or realize how far they have advanced to date, and not take firm action to stop them, *America will then become a Socialist Nation.*

Our Supreme Court agrees with the left on many issues. By president Obama's insertion of two more leftist progressive Judges into the Supreme Court, he has gravely shifted the balance of power to the Progressive left.

Their duty to interpret the law fairly, I feel, has been diminished. If this trend continues by either party, the purpose of our supreme court will be compromised, and soon, no longer be the respected body of our government it once was.

The Supreme Courts' explicit duty is to interpret the laws, and was put in place by our congressional body. Its responsibility was solely to investigate if the laws put forth, conform with our Constitution and Bill of Rights. There is to be no agreeing at all with any party or President.

Supreme Court Justices should be decided upon their knowledge of law as it would apply to our Constitution. It is also to give them the power by our Constitution to check the actions of the president and/or that of our Congress and Senate.

The Supreme Court has the final say in all cases involving the laws of Congress. However, the Court is not all powerful, it's power is limited by the other two branches of Government. It should never be persuaded or influenced by the President of either party that is in power at the time, or by the parties themselves.

I feel that the Progressives are poised and ready to move in to take over our nation very soon. Our next election is crucial to the existence of this free nation. Another leftist president may mean we have already lost our nation to socialism.

Our adversaries are not half a world away on the battle fields of Syria, Afghanistan or Iraq. They are here right now. They are mostly in the unions that are controlling our education system, the NEA, (The National Education Association), that can afford to spend huge amounts of money on electing officials they favor into our governing system, which they systematically have, over the many years of their existence.

They have contributed more money than labor federations, like the AFL-CIO. The largest campaign spender in the United States is not the Mega Corporations like Wal-Mart, Microsoft or Exxon-Mobil. It is not an industry association, like the National Association of Realtors or even the American Banker Association.

Take all the campaign spending of all the above entities and it will not match the amount spent by the National Educational Association to install a member of their choice into our Senate or congress.

The NEA, quietly spends heavily on campaigns that bring liberal candidates into our governing bodies. By doing this they gain control over candidates they helped, assuring the NEA, that laws that would benefit their union would pass, as was the case with teachers' tenure in Florida.

The democrats have been duped into being the pawns of this movement from way back in the early twenties, until this present day.

Over these many years, the progressives, I believe, have invested heavily into the democratic party. I imagine that the Fabian Society, through lobbyists bought the Democratic party with large donations, especially at voting times.

Large investments that were probably made, have caused Democrats to have no alternative at the present time, except to dance to the tunes of the liberals' progressive movement, not realizing that this is what they are doing, because they have been dumbed down for so many years of being their pawns.

If the Fabian society's progressive movement continues to successfully implement its plan to socialize our country, and if it is not realized by the voting public, and it may not be, because they have been lied to for so long, it will lead to the eventual loss of freedom for our country.

This would also affect the people of the rest of this world who may have aspired to become American's, and to be free.

Then never again will there be freedom or the hope of freedom for the people of this world. If the United States of America loses it freedom, the whole world will suffer.

Never again, will there be a nation that could offer true freedom that is found here in America. Once freedom is lost, no other government's communist, socialist, or the rulers of this New World Order would ever commit to a free society again.

For this is the very style of living they will destroy, in order to have control over the masses. Those in charge of this movement, the Fabian Society, do not care about freedom for the people under their rule.

The very first law that they will pass is to remove all guns from their people, because they know that weapons in the hands of the public, would be a hindrance to their cause.

We must come to realize that most of the nations in Europe have already succumbed to, or is about to become, socialized.

Is America also being forced into becoming a socialistic nation? Through a plan which started in England in the year 1884? I have no doubt that we are very close to losing our Constitution. President Obama's plan of taking from the rich and giving to the poor has quickened the pace of socializing our nation.

I believe that the whole of Europe can end up like Greece. That the Soviet Union will revive its communistic ways. Vladimir Putin is already taking steps in that direction, seeing how weak the United States has become under this present administration.

China will become much stronger. It too is already taking steps to strengthen its military. Cuba will remain at our doorstep, a stronger, more emboldened, communist country.

Socialism has already taken control of Great Britain, and has spread over all of Europe. America could be next. It is becoming very weak. If so, it will lose its power. A progressive form of Government will be in a position to take over our country.

Also, I believe that the populaces of this world will suffer drastically, masses of people on this earth will be living in poverty. Greece is an excellent example of what could take place if the rest of Europe did not pitch in to help them.

Imagine where the Greek nation would be under their present economic situation. Only because of the aid they are receiving from Germany and some other nations in Europe, are the Greek people not starving. The Greek country has turned into a welfare nation, their citizens have received so much assistance from their government, that they now actually refuse to work.

Their greatness was once part of their heritage. The magnificent Gods were once proudly respected throughout all of Europe. So great a nation in their time, has now been reduced to a pathetic socialist style of living.

How long can the rest of Europe keep supplying the aid necessary to keep the Greek nation alive? They, the rest of Europe, are on their way to becoming what the Greek people already have become.

Once Socialism gets a foothold on a country, the amount of all aid to their citizens is severely reduced. Greed of the people in power causes them to care less about the general Population. Cuba is a good example of the silent suffering happening to the people of that Communist nation.

The general public of Greece has little or no idea who the leaders of this progressive movement are, that have weakened them. I believe that they have no idea at all, except for the few who are at the very top of this movement, as is always the case, with the Fabian Society.

They operate silently and precisely. They know

their plan and carry it out efficiently to its conclusion.

They have advanced patiently, uninhibited over the last 120 years of their quest to have World dominance. The results of their effort is evident, throughout England and Europe.

They also, in the last 90 or more years, have made deep inroads into our government in the United States. Here in America, the liberal democrats have unknowingly been helping this Fabian movement infiltrate into our country for many decades.

I cannot understand why the Democrats cannot see the motive of this movement to change our country into a socialist nation. But then, the truth is hidden from them in order to keep them involved. I am not so sure that the Republicans can see what is happening either.

However, this growing cancer that has infected this nation continues to spread relentlessly, into every State, City, Town and Village of our land. Because of all the different liberal programs, social organizations and unions, that these socialists have formed over the last ninety years, has taken and continues to take its toll, on this, our Republic.

Every law given to us by our forefathers, to render the citizens of this nation, free of government, is constantly challenged. Our God given rights to pursue freedom and happiness is becoming more of a dream than a reality. We are slowly being transformed into living as slaves to an idea, that has been designed to destroy this once powerful nation.

Slowly but surely, we are giving up our unalienable rights, so thoughtfully planned for us by our forefathers.

At this present time in our history, what, in my opinion, is most important, is that our next president comes to terms with the fact, that our lesser enemies, are half a world away.

That the evil enemy that has engulfed us, that has been tormenting us, over this long period of time, is here, in the United States, ready to take control of our government, in order to take away our Republic.

The fighting that we are involved in, on foreign soil, is a war to be won. The fight at our door step is more crucial, it must be won to save our country.

Our nation has never faced so severe a challenge as we do now. The importance of all the people to unify to save our country is now.

When will the members of the Democratic party wake up and realize the dangers we face as a nation?

Have the Democrats any idea or even know, that there is planned takeover of this world. That they are the pawns being used to accomplish this mission by bringing down the United States? I believe not.

The United States is in a War with an invisible enemy. They have no real Army or physical fighting force, however, at the present time, they don't need one. They do have a plan in place, of world order, since 1884. I believe it is backed by billions of dollars that they have acquired through organizations that they installed into our governing bodies.

My hope is that I can convince the liberal Democrat's and Republican's, that this movement is real. It's now at a point where it is growing faster. Socialism over our Republic is coming to be.

Our Republic is in serious danger. Beware of Obama and the socialist cabinet that was formed under his presidential administration. Also, Bernie Sanders, who does not hide his socialist leanings behind the Democratic party as he used to.

The Progressive Fabian society movement must be stopped. The liberal left in this country have got to change and act on what is happening in America. I feel that Republicans are bogged down, as are the Democrats, and may also not be aware of this impending threat that hangs over America by the Fabian society's progressives' movement.

At the present time, this progressive movement has grown extremely large. They have, I believe, already engulfed the White House and put their people in top strategic positions in our government.

Also, at the present time, there are some that make up the president's cabinet, that do have a strong leaning towards socialism and communism.

This has become a serious problem under this administration. Neither party can take on this task alone. Without the Democrats full support, we may lose this crucial battle, and the United States will no longer be a free nation.

The progressive movement is very real! They have already, through their unions, taken over England and Europe, and are waiting in the shadows to move in on the United States. Their theory is that they can take over the world, without the physical strength of an army.

That nations can be taken over by methodologically attacking a government from within, weaken their economy, attack authority and create havoc, by demonstrating in the streets, in the towns and in the cities of a nation, all of which is happening in our country at the present time, unquestioned by anyone, especially in the liberal media.

We are sadly being taken advantage of, because our enemy has learned through our own laws, how to manipulate our Constitution and Bill of Rights, to their advantage. The law of America which permits free speech is greatly used to their advantage.

Let's not change our laws for anyone, ever! I'm sure, we as a free nation, can survive. We, as people that love this country, must be very careful who we vote in as our next president.

I feel that at the present time, we must keep a majority of conservatives in both houses, be they Democrats or Republicans, for as long as it takes to get this country moving in the right direction once more.

It could be very telling, if we get one more president like we have today. It would mean that our country has moved too far to the left. That it is then, only a matter of time for Socialist to sit at the helm of this great nation, and a slow decline in all that this Republic stood for, will eventually disappear.

Our country will no longer be the beacon of hope for this world. Where else can someone find a path to seek that would lead them to freedom? A freedom that has fueled the energy of men, only realized by Americans born to a truly free nation.

I believe that the future people of this nation, never again, will know what is to live free of oppression. We the people, will have been silenced forever. Instead, the government will show you what you can do or say. You will be living under social rule.

You will be stripped of all the laws that were there to protect you against a large government.

There will be no more rioters, no more demonstrations or protests, unless controlled by the government to prove a point. You will learn what it means to live in fear of your government. Hope of improving your life will no longer be in your control. You will unknowingly respond to the will of your new leaders of your government.

We must realize the severity of this impending danger that lies ahead. Telltale signs are when rioters boldly disrupt and disrespect authority. When they move beyond peaceful demonstrations into full blown riots, using any little excuse or reason to do so.

Their fearless attempts to attack the police of our nation is not always done spontaneously. It can be a well-planned timed attack, not only to disrupt authority but to instill fear in the minds of the public as well. Most importantly, it's a test to see the strength of their opposition or their willingness to fight back. Peaceful demonstrations in our country, are overseen by police and never interfered with, unless they become violent.

We have not seen many peaceful demonstrations in this country for a number of years.

Can we imagine a good reason why George Soros would pay marauders to invade our cities the way they did? He is not throwing his money away. Mr. Soros knows exactly what he is doing.

I sincerely wish that, we the people, would take the time and give some deep though, as to why Mr. George
Soros is doing what he is doing. How many other riots did he support in the past with his money?

How many more Police officers are going to be ambushed and killed, cars set afire and destroyed, small business's burned, forced to close, never able to open again? Were these marauders, also paid for by George? Why is Mr. Soros not being investigated?

He was and still is, a strong advocate of President Obama's political agenda. Our leadership can be corrupt and do know what lies ahead for this nation.

They are becoming bolder and more blatant in their activities, against us the people, and to the authority that is there to protect us. Does George care that his money could be aiding the attacks on our police? Can he be made accountable?

Think about what would happen to the demonstrators, if these demonstrations that we had recently in our country, took place in Communist nations. How would North Korea, China, Cuba, or even Russia, with Vladimir Putin in charge, deal with demonstrators?

They would be declared troublemakers, the enemy of the people. They would be corralled and killed. Shot where they stood, in the streets possibly, as a warning to their people, that such behavior will not be tolerated. Is this what the liberals Democrats want for our country?

This movement has been going on since 1884. We must realize that the original leaders are gone. So who are they, that are in charge now? This is not a movement to help the poor or the down trodden people of this world, though their propaganda will have you believe that they are, or to help the middle class or even the very rich.

Are the people in our nation on the left, or the Democratic liberals, that may know of this Fabian Society, and are still aggressively supporting this movement, do they think that they will benefit from it? I feel that if they do, they are sadly mistaken.

Only billionaires like George Soros can afford to support this movement. They, whoever they are, will not share, but will use, the many people involved, with empty promises.

But who are these people, and what can they gain, doing what they did in Europe? As of right now, the Fabian Society has control of the British Government and literally the European union. This is also what they are attempting to do here in America.

They are very skilled in their endeavor to influence certain men and women in high places, to follow them. But where are they going with this movement? Who will benefit by what they are attempting to accomplish?

This progressive movement if they are successful, will not be completed for hundreds of years. The people behind it now will be gone and they would have accomplished nothing at all for themselves. So why they are doing this, makes no sense at all.

Unless for the large amounts of money that is made with these liberal nonprofit organizations, that have been continually being supported by our government since they began. For years they continue to fill their coffers with our tax dollars.

All programs that they have in their control, bring in large sums of money, and they live on and are never investigated.

The ACLU receives more than a 120 Million Dollars yearly, mostly paid by the United States government from our taxes. Planned parenthood, is another program that receives huge amounts of money from taxes we pay.

The current president Cecile Richard as of 2006, has been receiving salaries that are in excess of $500,000 a year. She is a Democrat, was the founder of and became president of America Democratic Votes, a coalition of the national Democratic Party.

She was deputy chief of staff to the United States Representative Nancy Pelosi who was the leader in the United States house of Representatives. She worked at the Turner Foundation, in 1996 she founded "The Texas Freedom Network", a Texas organization that was formed to counter the Christian Right.

Planned Parenthood is active in various types of activities including Political Advocacy.

Cecile Richards married Kirk Adams, a Labor organizer with the Service Employees International Union, "SEIU". He left SEIU in 1989 to run Cecile Richards mother Ann Richards Gubernatorial Campaign and did so very successfully.

Planned Parenthood's annual report shows that they brought in $1.3 billion dollars in 2014. From sales of aborted baby body parts alone, they profit about $23 million dollars yearly.

While the liberal Democratic members of our government feel that we should continue to give half a million dollars of our tax money, yours and mine, to this organization, Planned Parenthood, on a yearly basis. Why?

These organizations continually do whatever they want, unchallenged. How can we call them a nonprofit organization? It has become larger than most of the profitable organizations in the United States. For years, they continue to do whatever they want, unchallenged, never any outcry from the liberal press. Why?

Because all of these organizations and unions, over many years, have grown so large. All were formed by the one group called the "Fabian Society" progressives movement. They have become larger, in my opinion, than any branch of our government.

They have a monopoly on the illegal sales of aborted baby body parts, a huge business and growing rapidly. They have been operating unchallenged by our law enforcer's for their illegal sales of baby parts for a very long time. And there is no outcry from the liberal press at all. Why?

With their control of the market on the sale of baby parts and the millions of dollars that are being made, I don't see them giving this money maker up very easily. They can well afford to spend millions on propaganda to keep it alive. Also, to encourage young women or unwed pregnant girls to abort their babies.

It all has been working so well for the liberal Democrat's for decades. I do believe that there are citizens of this country that are democrat's, and love this country as much as I do. I also truly believe that a majority of democrat's in position of power don't.

What they do love is the power and money they have given to themselves over the years. The money they spent to gain votes in their districts on all kinds of unnecessary projects that are paid for by taxing us.

But most importantly, the hundreds of billions of dollars given to all the nonprofit organizations which has an effect on all of us, both Democrats and Republicans alike.

The Democrat's, that are in positions of power, love to tax and spend other people's money. They seem to care less, that the more they spend, the more in debt America becomes. They know that it weakens us as a nation and strengthens the progressive movement, which they have been trained to favor.

It is why we have so many nonprofit organizations paid for with our taxes. When reviewing these organizations, none are in debt or are lacking funds.

They all appear to have billions of dollars at their disposal, that they have been successfully using to undermine our nation. I cannot understand how they can be classified as nonprofit.

Most of these nonprofit organizations historically date back to the 1920's and 30's or earlier. They came to be, about the same time the Fabian Society decided to make inroads into our government.

Over the years, through trial and error, they have learned how to use their evil ways skillfully, in their endeavor to socialize a nation.

They are patient, secretive and persistent in pursuing their goal of World Dominance. They use nonprofit organizations, like the EPA, to keep the general public busy, arguing over global warming or carbon monoxide contaminating our air. Or the ACLU having us, the public, divided over prayers in our public schools, or where we can display "In God We Trust".

They complain about allowing the nativity scene on certain pieces of properties, in specific areas of our cities, that it might be offensive to some, while they diligently advance their ideas of a new world order.

They, the progressive's, seem to have a nonprofit agency that can cover a multitude of issues, that can keep liberals and conservatives butting heads over long periods of time, while they serge ahead with their plans to dominate the world.

All of these issues, are just a few of many issues, that when settled in court are mostly won by the left, resulting in these NON PROFIT ORGANIZATIONS receiving large sums of money.

It distracts from the real issue of them secretly making inroads into our political system. All of this results in them being able to make generous donations to politicians to vote on issues that favor their cause.

If only the people of America, the movie makers and the liberal press, would stop letting themselves be used by the Fabian Socialist propaganda machine. If only they would realize that a movement has been put in motion by the Fabian's, and it has, and still is, happening in our country for over a 100 years.

Start to understand the danger of us losing our freedom. Stop and look at socialist countries. Pay attention to what is taking place China, Cuba, North Korea or Russia.

Understand how they force their people live. The oppression that is placed upon them, the fear they have of their governing body. Is this what we want for American's?

Let us return to who we really are! We are, The United States of America. We must stand united, bring all of our citizens together in this struggle to take back our country. Let's get away from party affiliation, to be able to unite and fight as a single unit, because this is the only way to defeat this evil cowardly enemy from across the seas.

The American people must be made to realize that the Fabian Society was formed in England. This is a foreign country to the United States. They have put together many programs to fight us in a very different type of war.

This is not a war against England, as was our war for independence against the British army in 1776.

It is a war to retain our freedom, that has now been put in jeopardy by an organization called "The Fabian Society Progressive Movement", and it is at our front door, waiting to enter.

Let us never forget, that it is a war that they have brought to our shores. It is no different than any other war. Their objective is to remove from us our inalienable rights given to all Americans from our forefathers.

Not having to deal with tanks, fighter planes or ships of war, does not mean that this is not a war. The consequences are the same. This is a war that must be won, or America as the free nation it is, will be lost and be gone forever.

This is not a war against another nation. It has been a war against an organization, that has been battling us, without any resistance from us, for about 100 years.

Because this fight was kept secret by our enemy, they have very skillfully been able to attack us in ways, that never in the history of this world, has ever been tried before.

They have fought us, having no boots on the ground, but with skilled lawyers at work, in courtrooms throughout our land, hard at work finding loopholes in our own laws.

They have been challenging our rights, given to the American people, by our Constitution, to maintain and keep our republic free of socialist rule. Their relentless attack, has been the only way for them to win. The time is now to stop them.

I would consider, that this is the longest war ever, that our nation has ever fought. Imagine, this war has been going on for over 90 years and they have been clever enough to not have us, their enemy, realize we are at war. I would say that more than 90% of Americans, have ever known that the Fabian Society even exists. But they do exist, they are real, and they are our enemy, that has us to the point of collapsing as a nation.

Americans must awaken to this reality and begin to fight back. We have to know our enemies in order to have a chance to win. Over the many years of them attacking us, we were led to believe that the opposing party was the enemy and kept us fighting each other. While they, the Fabian progressives, enriched themselves with our tax dollars, and now, it has become the most powerful force that the United States will ever have to engage.

It is a challenging fight, a war by their design that our enemy has created, not known to ever have happened before. This fight must happen, or our freedom will be lost.

On July 4th, 1776, we fought to gain our independence and we won. We had gained our freedom. We were at war with the British Empire, the most powerful country in the world at that time. They had a controlling interest in vast parts of this world.

Their army was well equipped and the best funded on earth. By comparison, the American army had a problem purchasing blankets and footwear for their men, yet the American's were successful against England in the war for independence.

They came here, into America, as a physical fighting force, to take our land from us. We fought them, man to man, and won. It was less than 15 years later, that our framers put together guidelines, to be followed by the men and women of this nation.

The framers were insisting that there be a guarantee that America would be a free nation for all of its citizens, to be clearly stated in a new born Constitution, and that our new government was to be strictly, for the people, and by the people.

Our strength would be sustained only if we remained united as a nation. It saddens me to realize that we are now divided, by an enemy that has kept us divided through their many liberal movements and various unions for more than 9 decades.

Start believing in our Constitution and our Bill of Rights once again, and realize how great a free nation, The United States, really is. It is our nation! We are the "United States of America". Let's take our country back!

Realize what is happening in our country, in our schools with our Board of Education. Why are students not learning about our forefathers or our presidents? Learn about our great generals, the pioneer men that died on farm land and the cotton fields of this country in battles fought.

A nation of men and women that died to preserve the rights of their fellow man. To allow the future generations to live free and enjoy their independence.

Our leaders, for so many decades, have let the progressives, this group of ruthless enemies, take apart our country. They have been chipping away at the very foundation of America, our Constitution, and our Bill of Rights, for over 90 or 100 years.

They get away with what they are doing to this nation unchecked or challenged, because they have already infiltrated into both the Senate, Congress and now our white house. Take a good look at the cabinet that he, Obama, has put together. You can tell a man, by the friends he keeps, for sure.

I remember as a boy, with school mates in class, all feeling so proud saluting our American Flag. Why is the pledge of allegiance not said at the start of each day, as it was in the 20'S and 30'S? Why isn't an American flag, in every classroom throughout our country, as it once was? Why, in our schools, over the last 75 years or more, have we stopped teaching, and are twisting the truth, about American History?

In God we trust, oops! - can't say that, cannot have that written on public or Government buildings inside or out, either. The ACLU said that it might be offensive to some.

Can't have a Nativity Scene displayed at Christmas time. That too, would dampen the feeling of those that may not believe in God. No prayers in schools - it would offend the children of atheists.

One child in class, complains that the prayer being said offends him or her and immediately the ACLU lawyers are in court and thirty-five or forty other students, or perhaps all students in every class room, in every school across America, must stop praying to their God.

All of this with the liberal school board agreeing,

going along with it, while the general public remains quiet, and the progressive movement moves on, unchallenged.

They can put 20 lawyers or more of the 200 plus lawyers that they have available to them, on any situation, or on what they may consider a problem, in a moment's notice, and at no real expense to the ACLU. The defense on the other hand, has very little at their disposal to fight with.

What I cannot understand is, why do we tolerate giving up what was accepted for hundreds of years by millions of people throughout this land, just to satisfy the will of a few.

This happens again and again, with many issues, and has been happening for many years in our courts. Why must the many, always capitulate to the few?

I would like to see more of these cases put to a national vote in the voting booth, instead of by trial to possibly liberal judges. Let's decide these grievances that they have with religion, our right to prayer, or any/all issues of this nature, by a vote.

Whenever there is a national election, a vote on these issues would then be decided in a fair and just way, by the majority of the American people. Not the over powering ACLU.

The ACLU is one of many similar organizations that have been formed over the years by the progressives' in this country. The ACLU, I believe, is the most powerful. They have over 200 staff attorneys at work, a well-trained, organized membership, of over 500,000 strong, and growing, with an annual budget of over a 100 million dollars.

They operate in all 50 states and Puerto Rico, ready to take on the smallest of grievances. With every case they win against our Constitution, they become stronger and the United States becomes weaker.

School unions have had a strong influence over "The Board of Education". Do we need unions in a position of influence enabling them control over our Board of Education?

Our School system was rated number one in the world of educators, in the 20'S and 30'S. With the progressive system of educating and now, along with union's controlling our teachers, our schools are now rated number 26. How then, are they of any help to our student body at all? They really don't care about the students.

I believe all unions are the strongest advocates of the Fabian Societies progressive movement. Their interests are far reaching. We must realize, that unions are grounded in a communistic philosophy.

It was easy for unions to convince liberal teachers to unionize.

This fit well into progressive's social agenda and over the years they managed to slowly and methodically dumb down the future citizens of this country, our children. Our children graduate from high school, with very little or no knowledge of American history.

That was a major subject in our schools in the thirties. Today, if American history is taught at all, it will convincingly be presented with lies about the greatness of America.

A math teacher, Albert Shanker, as a student, attended Stuyvesant High School in New York and the University of Illinois. Albert Shanker became a volunteer spokesperson for teachers that had some labor issues, with the Board of Education. Soon after that he formed a union called the "UFT", the United Federation of Teachers. Albert Shanker, started this union approximately thirty-six years ago, in New York city and its five boroughs. It has now grown to over two hundred thousand members.

However, the schools of this nation are already controlled by the progressive form of education. By adding the expense of unions to our school system, the cost of our education has slowly risen over the decades, increasing our school taxes, which impacts our cost of living.

This adds nothing to the quality of education for our children. How do we get control of this bad situation, that has been plaguing our school system for the last 90 years or more?

Whenever unions involve themselves into any form of industry, costs have to increase. The workers that unions organize get increases in salaries, which amount to very little. If you consider they have to pay union dues, higher taxes, along with paying into a higher cost of living, the gain the average worker receives is very little by comparison.

The added cost of taxes to the owners of businesses, corporations or industries, do not always impinge on their profit. It has the same effect that taxing the rich has. Owners of businesses pass the added cost on to the consumers, by raising prices, so the cost of living continues to rise.

When the liberal Democrats make claims that they are helping the poor by taxing the wealthy, they are being dishonest with the general public. They only are interested in getting your vote. In some cases, by raising the tax on the rich, the added costs of products, exceeds the amount of taxes that they might pay and the liberal left knows that.

The left cares less about the cost to the consumer, what they do know is, it always sounds good that they are taxing the wealthy. It brings in the votes, so the wealthy become richer and the poor become poorer and the progressive movement and unions gains more ground.

With smaller businesses in hard times, they in some situations, cannot always afford the demands of unions, causing them to close completely, putting their complete working force on unemployment.

It all comes down to the average worker's suffering the most. You won't hear much of that in the liberal press, they will not even be honest about the higher unemployment rate, especially when there are Democrats in charge of the white house.

At one time, unions did serve well in dismantling the sweat shops that were in New York and existed in other major cities across this nation. Times have changed, most business owners now realize, and it is proven, that the better workers are treated, the more productive they become. Back in the 20's, there were cases where unions were needed. Today they are not necessary at all.

It is my opinion they are out dated and have become an expensive part of our past. The example of how they have an over powering influence in our schools should raise a red flag, to teachers, principals or the Board of education, but nobody will ever complain, because of the liberal bias of the press or that of the televised news stations.

They are unified in their objective to have complete control over the student body and they do. Their plan is working and has been for many years. The left progressive's system has taken over the lives of our young.

They systematically are molding them into pawns, through their teachings, to become the future liberals in our society and to march, in lock step, with the many waves of leftist programmed students that came before them.

They have become the power behind the vote to change this nation into a socialist society and their battle is very close to being won.

Check to see if the teachers you know of lean towards the democratic and liberal viewpoints. I believe that you will find that an overwhelming number of teachers do. They feel free to do so, because they go unchallenged.

You will also notice that some teachers are very outspoken about their liberal views in their classrooms, without a counter argument from anyone. What they say becomes fact to the students in their classes.

They are your teachers! They have a strong influence over their student body. They are unionized and will follow the system, put in place, from the unions point of view, in their lectures to their students.

They, the teachers, were also students at one time and were subjected to same system that remains in place to this day.

So the cycle continues, more pawns are molded to carry out the progressive's socialist ideology. This movement becomes stronger with every day that passes. With every class that graduates.

It becomes amazing to me, that this has been going on for decades in our school system, with no one seeking to question, or bring attention to this taking place within our board of education.

Our Constitution has not been read in our schools for many years now. *Not read, taught or studied since the early 30'S, when the teachings of the progressive system took over our schools.*

Our Constitution, a set of rules, so well stated, so clearly written, so deeply infused with wisdom and common sense, that if followed, would be inspirational to be the goal of all people and of all the nations of this world. It clearly gives the power to the people. It is a guarantee, that as the population of our nation grows, the strength of the people also grows.

That as the laws of our nation, that gave just cause for our freedom to strengthen, would make it more difficult for governments to oppress its citizens. It asks for the citizens to be happy, prosperous and enable themselves, and the members of their families, to fulfill their goals, as proud Americans.

Can we imagine a government loyal to a socialist ideology, ask of its people, to be prosperous and happy?

Why would any nation not want this for their people? Why wouldn't the people of any nation, not want this to be their rule and be able to live under the conditions set forth in our Constitution?

To be free men and women having control of their own lives, that lets any nations people claim their God given unalienable rights to be free.

Carefully thought of and cleverly chosen words that would repave these roads that the down trodden and the poor of our world are forced to walk in despair.

The Articles of the Federation, the United States first governing document of 1776, was ill written and had left this young government weak. All states behaved like independent countries, without a president or judicial branch, and a congress that was ineffective. Congress was given the power to govern foreign affairs. It was also able to conduct wars and regulate currency, but it lacked the authority of enforcing any request for troops or money from the states.

After leading the continental army to victory during the American revolution, George Washington became a national hero. He was chosen, and voted in unanimously, to preside over the new governing document for the United States.

This important document, the United States Constitution, along with our Bill of Rights, established America's national and fundamental laws, which also guaranteed its citizens their God given basic rights.

The Constitution and the Bill of Rights, was known to be the oldest and shortest written Constitution, of any other major government in the world.

The Constitution was signed in Philadelphia, at Pennsylvania's State House, now known as Independence Hall.

The 1787 Constitution formed three branches of government with a system of checks and balances to assure that no individual branch could become too overpowering.

At the time of the signing of the Constitution, the population of the United States was about 4 million. It has been growing steadily over last 240 years, and now stands at 321 million. The word "Democracy", does not appear once in our Constitution.

All 13 states, except Road Island, sent a total of 55 delegates to sign the Constitution. Only 39 delegates eventually signed. Benjamin Franklin was the oldest to sign. He, at 81 years of age, was very weak and needed help to be able to sign and ratify the Constitution.

Also, because of illnesses, he had to be carried into the Pennsylvania State House, by four prisoners from the local jail house, in what was known as a sedan chair. It is said that, as he signed the Constitution, tears could be seen streaming down his face.

The youngest to sign, was a 26-year-old lawyer, named Jonathan Dayton, from New Jersey.

The United States Constitution was written during the convention in Philadelphia, from May 25th, to September 17th, in 1787. The framers of the Constitution, were a well-educated group of men. Many had served in the Continental Army. Among them were merchants, bankers, lawyers and farmers.

The U.S. Constitution needed 9 of its 13 state delegates to sign, in order to have this new law ratified. The first five were Delaware, Pennsylvanian, New Jersey, Georgia and Connecticut, in succession. Soon after, Massachusetts, Maryland and South Carolina signed. New Hampshire signed on June 21, 1788 to complete the nine states needed to ratify the Constitution.

The framers said, after the Constitution was ratified in 1788, was this quote:

"It would be necessary, that government, to secure these rights, men are to receive just power with the consent of government. That if any form of government becomes destructive of these ends, it becomes the right of the people, if necessary, to abolish or alter it. A new government is to be installed having principals based on a strong foundation. It shall organize its power in such form, so to affect the safety and the happiness of its people. It should be established, that our government should not be changed for light or transient causes".

George Washington was the first to sign, on the day it was presented, the 17th day of September 1787. When he was asked what his thoughts were, he replied – "Appears to me to be a little short of a miracle".

When John Adam was asked, he said, it was the greatest single effort of national deliberation that the world has ever seen.

As Benjamin Franklin left the Pennsylvania State House, after the final meeting of the Constitutional Convention on September 17th, 1787, the wife of the Mayor of Philadelphia approached Benjamin Franklin, curious about the new Government and asked what it would be? Franklin replied; *"A Republic Madam, if you could keep it."*

Two hundred and forty years ago, Benjamin Franklin told the Mayors Wife of Philadelphia that we have a Republic if we could keep it. Well so far we have kept our Republic, but will we and for how much longer?

Just imagine 6 sheets of parchment, that of which has on only 4 of its pages, 4200 words that were some of the most powerfully though out words ever written. These thoughts that came out of the minds of these brilliant, caring men of that era, was to assure that the men women and children of this great nation would be born free and remain free.

That the people will be the strength that guides this country, not that our government is to ever become the controlling factor in the lives of the people. Guided by the wisdom of this simple idea, a concept of what true freedom could be for its people, was born.

Our Constitution so carefully laid out a set of rules and laws, that has a binding effect on the lives of the citizens of our nation to this day. Inspirational words that were penned by our framers to firmly unite our country, for the framers of our Constitution knew, that united we shall stand, if divided we would fall.

These words gave little or no doubt at all to the idea, that a nation was being developed, that which the strength of this nation would be on the reliance of its people and not its government.

This proved to be an accurate assessment that has served us well for many long years. Let us fight not to lose what is a precious gift from our forefathers.

Also, that freedom was the right of every living citizen living on this land. That this quest for freedom would be realized and remain in the control of the people of this great nation forever.

Also, that the strength of these written words has proven to be the inspiration, the reason, that the United States of America is the strongest and the most powerful nation that has ever existed on this planet earth.

Our Constitution has given us a fair and honest approach to govern its people. Also, to instill in the people that have come to us from all parts of this world, seeking to be free of oppression. To become citizens of this great nation, I would imagine, to have on this planet earth, a truly free country, that America has proven to be, was a dream that came true.

Well, I now believe, that our nation is in a serious crisis. I honestly believe that, this once powerful nation, has been weakened drastically. Our America now stands divided because of men like president Obama and his socialist communistic cabinet in our White House.

Al Sharpton, makes speeches to divide, disrupt, and destroy neighborhoods.

George Soros, a billionaire, has paid marauders, millions of dollars, to riot and destroy property, causing billions of dollars in damage to innocent shop owners of small businesses and George is not held accountable.

A nation that had fought evil whenever, or wherever it raised its evil head, but now appears helpless to defend itself against the evil, this relentless cancerous evil, that has been planted into the core of our nation, growing without any resistance within the confines of this country's borders, since the early twenties.

Why can't the majority of the democratic party, or the liberal left, understand what history has been telling us for hundreds of years, that not any form of social government or dictatorship has ever succeeded. In the process to succeed, there is an ongoing suffering to the oppressed people of their nations.

The general public under this progressive ideology, or any other form of socialist type of government, are under the strict and dominant control of their leaders. Their citizens will never live free. They live in fear of being sent to jail, or even put to death, if caught breaking any of their social laws.

Why would any government want this for their people? How they can go on not caring, can only be attributed to the evil greed of their leaders. For them to achieve their world order, they cannot tolerate protests and planned mayhem that riots cause. But, it is exactly what they are free to do in a Republic society, that they have been successfully using here in order to take over our country.

If the progressive movement did take over this country, the first people that they would put in jail or kill are the demonstrators. I believe, that the last thing they would want to have to deal with, are the demonstrators. They know that they are paid troublemakers and could be a problem to their movement in the future.

In the past, whenever there was a forced change of government, there was a mass slaughter of people that takes place with it, as it happened in Russia with Joseph Stalin and in China with Mao Tse-Tung.

Over the last two hundred and forty years, of the United States existence, since our Constitution was written and put forth, it has given us a strong foundation to support a free nation that has outlasted most other forms of governing bodies in this world.

With our governing Republic, our Constitution and the strength of our Bill of Rights, we have successfully outlasted most forms of governments in the western world.

The duration of their power, wherever the communist or the Fabian Society has planted a socialist form of government, it has not lasted very long.

To mention a few main governments are:

1. The Soviet Union - from Dec. 30th, 1922 to Dec. 26th, 1991 - a reign of 69 years. Stalin had killed

six million of its citizen's to do so, much less than the 20 million previously thought.

2. China - to date, 68 years. Mao Tse-Tung caused 40 million of its citizens to die with his failed plan, "China's great leap forward", as it was named, was a disaster.

   The people, being under the control of so ruthless a leader, remained powerless to even protest. For anyone to rise out of the shadows to speak, would be silenced by the fear of severe reprisal.

3. North Korea - to date, 67 years in power.

4. Cuba - to date, 56 years in power, all with deaths on their hands.

Realizing that these nations have existed for many years prior to them becoming Socialistic societies, as Monarch's or Dictatorship's, their present reign of power were and are quite short.

Russia, as an example, was not at all successful either. The only thing that was evident, was that the people living in those Socialist societies lived in fear of their government constantly.

They knew that if they disagreed with their leaders that only punishment would ensue.

That the people that were, or that are still trapped in these forms of government suffer greatly at the hands of their leadership.

If we can understand that socialist governments have very little regard for their people, their main concerns are for themselves and those that ride the crest of socialism with them.

They claim to be voted in and that the people want them, but we know, along with the voting public, that their voting machines are corrupted, and are fixed to change their vote.

I suspect that was the case with "Acorn", during our own presidential election, especially in 2012. Acorn! They were recruiters of voters. They recruited the same voters over and over again then took them to other locations to vote some more.

They were busing them into different states to continue to vote over and over again. I cannot tell you how many times Mickey Mouse voted, or other cartoon characters, that pulled the voting leaver to vote Democratic.

They take no chances. They know an honest vote would rule them out. If there is pain or suffering for the people under their control, does not bother them at all.

Their concern is the power and the riches that come with power. They rule with an iron fist and a smile on their face, without fear of reprisal, because they have laws that have strict control over the people and all weapon's.

All socialistic society's will never, as it is allowed here in America, let their populous own even a pea shooter. Socialists know that they are disliked by their general public. They take no chances in being shot. The punishment for owning firearms would be extremely harsh.

I would like the citizens of America to hear what President Obama, Hillary Clinton, and the rest of the left are saying about our gun laws. They are trying to convince the citizens of this nation, that most of crime in our country is caused because of our laws that permits us, the people, to own guns.

They know that is not true. They claim that if we remove all the guns from the people, there would come an end to all the murder that has been happening in our schools and places where crowds congregate. And they know that is not true.

Also it would put an end to all murders in the streets of major cities. That also is not true, and they know that, which in most cases, the shooters were mentally deficient.

They know that these surprised or unprovoked attacks would be difficult to detect or stop, or that the shooting was an act of terrorism.

They also know that any law passed to remove guns from the people, will only be obeyed by the honest citizens who will always obey the law.

They know that it would be impossible to keep weapons out of the hands of criminals. Immediately, when these unfortunate crimes occur, they jump on it and turn it into a political issue.

Obama recently declared that it should be a political issue. The shooting of black on blacks, which has been happening in Chicago almost daily, never seems to come to the table, or when our police officers are ambushed and murdered in sneak attacks throughout America. Not a word is to be said from the left, Hillary or our President Obama. **WHY!**

There is very little outcry from the left, or from Hillary or Obama. Why! Because I believe, they are lying to the American people, and they know that they are.

This is no surprise with this administration, it has been a continuous pattern of lies from people that have all of their citizens' lives at stake. They know that by changing our gun laws, this will not curb the crime one bit.

Their concern is not at all about the crimes that are being committed. It is almost as though they are happy to have a reason to declare their justification to remove all guns from what could become the fighting public from those of us that have the desire to save this nation.

It is very important to the Fabian Society's desire to change this country to a socialist nation. The changeover would happen much smoothly if the citizens are disarmed, and they do know, that is truth. All the people of all the nations, under the rule of communism or that of socialism, are forbidden under penalty of law, to own guns.

That's because they also know, that for the progressive movements effort to take control of this government, is not the will of the large majority of the American people, and a battle could ensue.

They, without an army, could lose this war that they have brought to the American people over 100 years ago.

But all of the American people must be made to understand the great danger we are facing. All the people of both parties have to be convinced that this threat is real. It already has taken place in

Great Britain and all of Europe and it is very close to happening here in America.

It is a fact that any major meetings or critical decisions that would take place, or be made in Great Britain or Europe's governments, the presence of members from the Fabian Society is required. If this is the case, the governing body of these nations have lost control, that the true leaders are then the Fabian Society.

This next election is critical to the very existence of our nation. Our country, to remain a republic, is at stake.

Please take the time to research what I am writing about. I have and it scares me. America is a wonderful nation, and our government has been, until recently, the most honest and fairest to its citizens, then any government ever, any place in this world.

The members of our present government now continually lie and deceive the American people whenever the need is there, to advance their socialist programs, and it is done with a smug attitude. They know that they have the unconditional support of the liberal press and the backing of all the socialist led organization's that were put in place by the Fabian society's progressive movement.

This nation, to survive, needs to realize we are about to lose our freedom. Our enemy, is this massive movement taking place, to move our country into a Socialist State, resulting in the destruction of the United States.

It is a battle for the life of America. It is no different than being at war. A silent war that they brought to us, is still a war.

To overcome what is happening, we the people of these United States, need to start fighting back. We must declare war on the enemies among us before it is too late.

We, next year, have a very important election coming up. I am sure that Acorn will be involved. Perhaps not as Acorn, but under a new name. Their corrupt goal's will always be the same.

How can we be sure of what the extent of their involvement will be in our election process? It is difficult to access, but I am sure it will go on unimpeded. I would like to see more of an outcry from the fair minded citizens of this country.

In 2004, in the state of Washington, the Secretary of State, described Acorn's illegal activities as the, "Largest case of voter fraud in the state's history." Cases of voter fraud was found in other states as well, including Missouri and North Carolina.

Acorn gained strength in 1970. To become a leftist group, President Obama's ties to this organization began with Acorn's president, a woman named Madeleine Talbot. When Obama was in Chicago, at that time, as an organizer, he was asked and did give many lessons on the subject of leadership and organizing to Acorn.

However, Obama claims that he never worked for Acorn, but Obama failed to report that in 2007 he gave Acorn $800,000 dollars from his campaign coffers. Imagine this huge sum of money given to Acorn just before the 2008 election.

Are we in the United States, now fixing our elections? Is this the nation we have become? Has the left made it impossible for America to have a fair and honest election? How can we be sure, our next election will be an honest projection of what the majority of our voters want? We can't.

What does it take for people to see, that when the left has a problem that may confront them, they form an organization, secure the support of government and continue to grow?

Acorn is a good example. Can you imagine having a force the size of Acorn working on the behalf of liberal causes generating votes to bring more power to the left.

There is no Republican's defense to balance these unfair practices. They are relentlessly persistent, unchallenged, because the power the left has put together through there many organizations.

Acorn with their 400,000 membership, lobbied for liberal causes, the raising of minimum wages, and universal health care. The reason for this is that they know it will bring in votes from the poor among us. They have no concerns for the down side of these causes, or the poor at all. Their fight to bring socialism to America, is all they care about.

I do not believe that any president, since the Fabian progressive society, started to form its organizations in the United States, some being formed before the nineteen twenties and after, have made any effort to really study what they were about.

Acorn, the EPA, ACLU, CPC, Planned parenthood, global warming, the many unions whose membership lobbying for liberal causes and I imagine there are many more leftist programs, that may not be listed above, are not only to secure voters, they also are lobbyists, for only and all liberal causes.

They, the Fabian society, shrewdly started with programs that appeared to be helpful for the people of our nation, but slowly and surely they will stomp on our Constitution and Bill of Rights.

These organizations, they claim, is from donations and also from philanthropists. However, they also were able to be funded by the American Government, costing the tax payers many billions of dollars.

The people that are in charge of these organizations, do lean strongly to the left. The cures for complaints that they have, somehow always seems to be, to the detriment of this country.

The Environmental Protection Agency, "the EPA" by imposing stringent rules and regulations, most times unnecessarily, doesn't do any good in protecting the air we breathe. I doubt very much, that the rules imposed on businesses to protect the environment here in the USA, are very effective. They have little or no effect at all.

Most rules can and do, add extra costs, that slows down production, leading to increased costs for the consumer and also causing, in some cases, businesses to reestablish themselves in other countries.

Unless India, China, or other cities in the world, conform to the rules imposed by the EPA, the global effect is little to none. It is my opinion, the

EPA knows that, and they also know that their clean air plan is not that efficient either.

This is a liberal organization, their objective is to hinder, not to help, in any way, the growth of this nation's business's.

They, like the many other organizations developed by the Fabian society's progressives' movement, is to change this nation from being a Republic, to Socialism. Making the United States part of a world order. Again, they shrewdly get tax dollars, to use against and bring harm to our government.

The Congressional Progressive Caucus "CPC", is the largest membership organization within the Democratic Caucus in the United States Congress, with seventy-six members. They, being democrats, is a farce. They are socialists, there again a lie.

They are hiding behind the democratic label. There is no honesty among these people, all is fair if it helps their cause. If they are not truthful as to who they are, they will not be honest about what they will do.

These congressmen lean heavily to the left, it works to advance liberal and progressive issues and positions. They are involved with and possibly are members of the Communist Party, USA.

The CPC, is co-chaired by US Representatives, Democratic Raul Galvani of Arizona, and Keith Ellison, Democrat of Minnesota. CPC has added twenty new members since 2005. A growing socialist movement, that can be seen growing in our country, is frightening.

CPC was founded by Bernie Sanders in 1991, a self-proclaimed socialist. The CPC organization has been growing steadily since its inception, to the point where Bernie Sanders, has now gained the confidence to run for president of United States as a Socialist, not as a Democrat.

The Congressional Progressive Caucus, CPC, is the socialist wing of the Democratic Party. It's members in congress keep close ties with the institute of policy studies and the Democratic Socialists of America. It also has ties with the "Communist Party USA."

Bernie Sanders served in the House of Representatives from 1991 to 2007, and has served in the United States Senate since 2007. (Look up "Bernie Sanders" on AOL.)

Planned Parenthood, was founded by a woman named Margaret Sanger. She was originally the founder of an organization called the American Birth Control League. The ABCL, in 1921, evolved into "Planned Parenthood" by 1928. She was Marxist orientated, and also a feminist advocate of eugenics and forced sterilization.

Margaret Sanger was born on September 14, 1879, and died in Tucson Arizona nursing home on September 6, 1966. (She also can be researched on AOL.)

It is worth knowing the minds of the organizers of these different leftist organizations. These people that have so much control over the lives of so many citizens of America, and for so many decades, are endorsed by the socialist Democrats in our congress and senate. They continually choose to support and vote to fund these organizations, and with our tax dollars.

This is not what our forefathers wanted for America and its citizens. It is within our right, that we the people, put a stop to all of these Liberal leftist organizations.

We have the majority in both houses. We need a strong President that knows who our real enemies are, and who begins to dismantle them, as quickly as possible. A president who knows evil that has grown inside the structure of our nation and is affecting the lives of all Americans. Who gave these people the right to do this damage to our country? We must stop them before it becomes too late.

Planned Parenthood - what a disgraceful group of individuals. They have discredited themselves severely. Not only do they get tax dollars from our government, but they encourage and help women get abortions, and then sell body parts from the aborted babies. How disgustingly low can you get? There never is an outcry from the liberal press. Why?

To what level of disgrace, do the liberals want to bring this nation down to? Is this what we want the rest of the world to see? This is the lowest form of genocide ever. How can anyone end a life of a baby and profit from their demise.

This is another left liberal group that bends to the will of the progressive movement.

Some of these leftist organizations have engulfed this country for the last ninety years or more. I understand, there can be prevailing circumstances for aborting an embryo, but to carry a baby to term, abort the infant and carefully remove body parts to sell, is the ultimate in horrendous crimes.

It was shocking to listen to Carly Fiorina describe this on the CNN Republican debate, held on September 16, 2015. She described how a baby, with heart beating and feet kicking, was lying on a table while a decision to keep the infant alive was being made, as to how to remove the brain of this aborted child.

She was adamant about President Obama and Hillary Clinton, to watch that disgraceful video. How can they continue to stand with Planned Parenthood? An organization, who's horrendous criminal behavior that has, I would say, resulted in murder. Will the people that preformed this abortion be held accountable?

How can any person, especially those that have children, that have held a new born baby in their arms, see how helpless they are, stand there and ponder on a way to safely kill a baby to salvage the child's brain?

Can we really imagine how the minds of some, be so unfeelingly void of emotion, that are so sadistically driven to be able to perform so hideous a crime. Then to be able to close their eyes at the end of a day and have a peaceful night's sleep? How unfeeling and cold heartened are members of this organization? Where are we? In Nazi Germany? Any government that can let this happen should hang their heads in shame.

The American Civil Liberties Union, the ACLU, is a leftist secular progressive organization. An American, named Mr. Roger Baldwin, helped form the ACLU in 1920, along with Crystal Eastman and several others. He was in charge of the ACLU for the first 30 years.

Mr. Roger Baldwin was a supporter of Communism, but he did denounce it later on. It was stated in his book, *(A New Slavery),* which condemned *"The inhuman communist police state of tyranny."*

The ACLU had and still has a leftist agenda. One that censors' prayer, and also the recognition of God in public schools or institutions.

Rodger Baldwin, in 1935, fifteen years later, sought the total destruction of the United States. This man, Roger Baldwin, was proud of his soviet style of Communism. He later proved to be the greatest influence in bringing communism to our United States and into our legal system. As leader of the ACLU, he permitted the entry of many Communists into the organization.

At that time, Baldwin wrote, *"I am for Socialism, disarmament and ultimately, for the abolishing of the State itself. I seek the social ownership of property, the abolition of the propertied class and the sole control of those who produce wealth. Communism is the goal".*

He also wrote, in his book, "Liberty under the Soviets", the following, *"I don't regret being a part of the Communist tactic which increased the effectiveness of a good cause. I knew what I was doing. I was not an innocent liberal. I wanted what the Communists wanted!"*

His goal was to affect an increase of communism into his organization. He became very successful in accomplishing that goal. This enabled him to continue his anti-American propaganda, with inhabited strength, and he has unfortunately, done just that.

Rodger Nash Baldwin's endeavors, are clearly described in a great article, very clearly written by author Sher Zieve, **"Dismantling the USA, Part 1: The beginnings"**. (Search the Web).

Mr. Anthony D Romero, was born in New York, on July 9, 1965, to Puerto Rican parents. He is a self-proclaimed homosexual. He became CEO of the ACLU, and presently is in charge of running this organization since September 2001. He has continued in the footsteps of Rodger Nash Baldwin.

This organization, over the many years of their existence, has been relentlessly seeking the destruction of these United States of America.

We cannot continue to let this movement advance unabated. Strong measures must be put in place to stop the Fabian societies progressive movement in this country. We, as a unified nation, both

Republican and Democratic, must stand together to change our direction. Stopping America from turning into a Socialist nation, must become our goal.

It is my opinion, that our next president, man or women, Democrat or Republican, must have a strong will and understand the need to protect our Constitution and ensure that The Bill of Rights is enforced as the only laws of this great nation. To make America great again.

A little less than a 100 years ago the Fabian Society had decided to take control of America. A silent war was declared by them against the United States of America. Sneakily, covertly and extremely persistently, they managed to use our laws to change the direction of our country.

What they have in store for us will be the complete destruction of this nation, and their mission is very near to completion.

We in America, must realize that they have declared this war, and the weapons used by them are the many organizations' that they have formed to facilitate this battle. I believe that it would be in the legal interest of our country to dismantle these leftist organizations weapons, one by one, because written in our Constitution, that I have quoted here, and earlier, was what was said by the framers of our Constitution.

They have made it very clear.

"It would be necessary, that government, to secure these rights, men are to receive just power with the consent of the government. That if any form of government becomes destructive of these ends, it becomes the right of the people, if necessary, to abolish or to alter it. A new government is to be installed having principals based on a strong foundation. It shall organize its power in such form, so as to effect the safety and happiness of its people. It should be established, that our government should not be changed for light and transient causes".

We must understand, that we, as citizens of a free nation, have the right to remove by law, any restrictions that would place the freedom of the people in jeopardy, or otherwise remove from the people, their inalienable right in the pursuit of their goal to seek happiness.

This has been happening to the members of our American society over many decades. The public has not been aware of this, because of the methods used by the Fabian society. They became extremely clever over many years of trial and error to hide their true motive.

They know that the plan they have for The United States, is only for their benefit, and also to quicken their evil takeover of this nation. Everything they do, is to take complete control of our government, and to eventually be able to complete their mission of ruling the entire world.

They have declared war on the United States close to 100 years ago. They have made us their number one enemy. Let us never, not believe, that we have not been deeply involved, in a bitter long planned war, and by a cowardly enemy.

Our enemy, the progressive movement, that was able to hide the truth as to what really has been taking place here in America. That they have been fighting us, under the cover of many shrewdly designed organizations. Cleverly hidden, planned and executed under the direct guidance of their Army of lawyers.

Lawyers compiled over a period of a 100 years or more, well trained professional men and women, put together to carry on the necessary steps in the pursuant of their goals - to ultimately bring socialism to America. The conquest of the United States of America is of utmost importance in their quest to dominate the World.

Make no mistake, the United States is at War. We must recognize it for what it is, or we will not be able to win this important fight for our very existence as a free nation. It is the most serious war our country has ever been involved in.

The Fabian Society is an extremely capable fighting force. They were able to keep hidden from America this on-going battle. A fight they have been having with the United States for close to 100 years. Keeping it secrete, has rendered us defenseless against our enemy.

The time is now to realize the impending danger we are facing. That this is a war, that we must engage in and must use every weapon at our disposal to win, for our survival as a free nation is at stake.

America must take certain steps to maintain freedom for its people. We have no choice, except to dismantle every organization that they are or have been using, in this fight against us.

I would say that all their organizations, the labor unions they have formed, all school unions, teachers and professors, are to be considered fair game. This war that we must engage in, is to correct all of the damage they have unjustly brought to our nation, and for so long a period of time.

Our next president should write out a declaration of war against The Fabian Organization. He or she should put together a team of the smartest lawyers in this country, and use as many as it will take to investigate all activities that the Fabian society is or was ever engaged in, over the many years that they have been fighting this battle to take control of our country.

The damage they have brought to this country over the many years that they had declared this war against us, is impossible to evaluate. They, the many organizations that they have created, whose sole purpose is to unfairly remove from the citizens of this country, their inalienable rights.

We should freeze all their assets if found guilty of the treasonous or of any crimes against our country. We should confiscate all their bank accounts, fine them heavily and put the people in charge in jail. A deep vigorous investigation of all the union organizations and especially school unions and the teachers themselves, should be scrutinized.

Every effort should be made to bring our nation back to where we were before we were attacked by the evil forces of this Fabian Society's progressive movement, nearly one hundred years ago.

I cannot express enough the importance of the steps, we as a nation, must take to keep our freedom, save ourselves as individuals, and to hold onto our Republic. The time to act is now.

The glory of our nation should be upheld. Our God given rights as stated in our Constitution is to be, for the people, of this great country. To also be instituted, by the people. No other force should be allowed to remove from us our unalienable rights.

There cannot be a pursuant of happiness given to the people of America by our forefathers, under the rules that will be set forth under a socialist government.

We Americans, were guaranteed freedom, only if we could hold on to our republic, as Benjamin Franklin so clearly stated to the governor's wife of Philadelphia over 240 years ago.

Without interference from an outside force, the United States grew steadily into a proud and powerful nation as proven in the first world war. The might of any other nation to challenge America was not there.

Only in the last 90 years or more, the strength of America is being weakened by the relentless discrediting of our values, by members of our own society, organized through a plan designed not by any country, but by a group of people under the name of the Fabian Society progressive movement.

A strong effort to save our Republic must become our number one priority, if America, as our forefathers so cleverly planned for us, is to be restored as the greatest nation that ever existed on the face of this Earth.

This can only happen, if our next election brings to power a man that is seeking to bring greatness back to America, to the level that America once had, once again.

May God Bless AMERICA.

Part 2

IMIGRATION AND OUR BORDERS

Europeans arriving here in the United States, at the turn of the 20th century, were made to stop at Ellis Island to be cleared for entry into this country.

Most were poor, in search of a new life, with the possibility and dreams of prosperity and, I imagine, a desire to feel free.

They came to America from countries throughout the world, men and women of all ages, in search of a better life for their families and themselves.

Most immigrants that came from Europe arrived at Ellis Island in New York harbor. There, they were given a physical, and were registered before entering the streets of New York, probably scared and confused, not knowing what lies ahead. Most of them had no relatives here to pave the way for them.

They were alone and on their own, facing a new life in a strange land. There were no handouts, they had to find a way to make a living or starve. They had very little choices, and they had to do everything in their power to survive.

The immigrants worked hard and applied their trades. They used their skills to forge a new life in a new world. They heard of a great new world where the opportunity to advance their lives was available to them. They no longer had to suffer the oppression they suffered in their native lands.

They were proud and happy to be in the USA. The will to survive was there! And the place to do it was here, in a land that was free, called America.

It was before the first world war, when there was a large influx of immigrants that ventured into this new world. America was a growing nation in need of the skills that the immigrants brought with them to our shores.

To learn to speak our language was one of the most difficult problems for them, but the courage that brought them to America, gave them the strength to overcome most obstacles that they would face. To speak English was only one of them.

The immigrants also brought many different styles of living when they emigrated to America. There were many different ethnic groups that came from many different places of Europe and Asia. The people colonized and formed neighborhoods in different cities throughout the United States. Often, they held onto their traditional values and styles of behavior of their native land.

This created a very pleasant atmosphere. We were able to visit different neighborhoods, learn to appreciate their customs, and enjoy the taste of foods that was native to the country they came from.

There was a strong effort to hold on to their heritage. Family roots were and still are very important to people of all nationalities, even today. Some of us are constantly searching for the roots of our family names and information about when their names were first established.

The immigrants that followed after the world wars had a much easier passage into the USA. The families who came here later knew people here. They had friends, and some had families who had come here many years before. This minimized their struggle.

In some cases, the groundwork was planned, laid out for them in advance. They had a place to go and a chance to adjust to their new environment. Some even had jobs waiting for them.

No immigrant I have ever spoken to, ever expressed regrets for coming here. Rather, they were very excited to be here and extremely thankful for the opportunity given to them by this great free nation.

This free nation, the United States of America, was founded on a strong and well thought out, Constitution and a Bill of Rights. After living under the laws that were framed by our forefathers, realizing the freedoms that have been put forth and written into our constitution. It was a remarkable change in life style for new comers to this land seeking to become citizens of this great country.

The freedom of speech, to speak your mind, express your thoughts without being oppressed, especially from the fear of government's intervening into a person's life. The comparison of the lifestyles alone, from where they came, to where they have come, gave strength to the desire to work hard in achieving a better life.

After living under the umbrella of our Constitution and guided by the laws of our Bill of rights. To have a government under the control of its citizens, as was its design, planned by our framers. Why would anyone want to live under the dark shadows of Socialism?

But there is a force that wants to bring drastic change to our United States of America. For approximately 100 years now, the Fabian Society has been making a strong effort to change America into becoming a socialist country. Not many citizens of America are aware of this taking place, or even heard of this progressive movement, that has been, for many decades, trying to change the course of our country.

This is no longer a threat, this is a reality. It is at a point where it could happen very soon. Unless we believe that this is taking place and start a counter action, our freedom will be replaced with The Fabian Society's type of socialism. It will be a sad moment for America.

To lose what our forefathers gave us, will be the end of our freedom and the hope of true freedom for all the civilized people of this world. There is a movement happening in this country to alter, discredit, or even remove our Constitution. This powerful document showed the world how important it is to live as a free people.

For about the first 130 years since the signing of our Constitution into law, did the people of this country experience the real meaning of freedom. It was about 1920 when the erosion of our Constitution had slowly begun.

It was then, when the Fabian Society started to engage in tactics to discredit our laws, in order to strengthen their position with the New World Order. They have been picking our laws apart ever since.

Our Constitution, I believe, has been the best

document ever written, not only for Americans, but for all the peoples of this world. It opened their eyes to what it would mean to be free of government. This is so hard to attain once government has dominance over its people.

Having voted into office the wrong people to lead us, will only add to the tragedy of us losing our freedom. In recent years, we have more or less, been on a serious decline. If we are not careful, this possible loss of freedom will definitely become a reality.

From the onset of humans on this earth, people of all ethnic groups, throughout the world, continue to want to better themselves. Knowledge of a land, where the people were in charge of their government, by written laws, allowing them a truly honest approach, to be the governing factor in their own lives.

As ruled by the majority of its citizens, more than just an idea, but as a rule of law, stated clearly in a Constitution with a Bill of Rights, now enforceable by law, encouraged a huge influx of people to want to become citizens of America.

Back in the late 1800s, the immigrants now knew and believed that America was the land of the free. It was a place where they would be able to improve their life, where hard work was rewarded, enabling them to earn a good living.

Their family was extremely important to them. They were a proud people that appreciated their new found independence and freedom. Just to be here, in the United States, to most, was in itself, a great achievement.

Also important to them, was their bloodline, and they wanted to keep it as pure as they could. Often, marrying outside of their religion or nationality was forbidden. This was only by their own desire. It was not at all instituted by our government.

Sadly, we are losing the stability of the family unit, which is so important to the connection of our past of who we are and where we came from. We are losing the strong basic foundation that generates a strong family.

A child having both a mother and father is so very important for the child's growth. There is a feeling of security and confidence that strengthens the bonds of a complete family unit. Knowing that their basic family foundation is solid, also gives support to a strong society.

There are far too many families with children who do not know who their fathers are. With mothers, incapable of giving proper care to children born out of wedlock.

I understand that in some communities the families absent of a father in a household is 80 percent. I am sorry to say, that welfare has given many, a free lunch. The price we pay, may one day destroy this free nation. This free lunch may be the price we pay in exchange for our freedom.

Today the majority of immigrants that come here, are from South America, mostly Mexican. Approximately 11 million are here illegally. I have heard that there could really be as many as 18 million illegal aliens here who have crossed our borders.

I would imagine that most people would welcome them with open arms, if they went through the proper channels to come here. The effort our relatives had to go through, by order of a set of rules, presented to them, laws that had to be obeyed, to become a citizen of America. This does not seem to apply to them. We may one day suffer the consequences of our loose borders. This might do unrecognizable harm to this nation, if this trend continues.

I have no proof, if what I am about to write, is really happening. It is all speculation. I only see this as a possibility. I have a fear that it can happen, because of the loose borders that we have lived with for the last 25 or 30 years or maybe more, and the refusal of the Democrats, the liberal left, and also our current president, to even consider to do something about it. So my fear is as follows.

If among the 11 million illegal Mexicans that crossed our boarders, over the past 25 or 30 years, Jihad trained terrorists may have entered with them, numbering in the thousands!

It's difficult for me to prove, but if true, in all 50 states, they could have cells of highly trained terrorists. I believe that illegal aliens have been crossing our borders for more than 30 years. Terrorists could be poised and waiting, this very moment to attack us.

If this is true and they placed themselves in strategic locations in each of our states, waiting for orders to attack at a given time we, at once, would be for the third time in our history, facing our enemy, in battles on the city streets of our nation.

With most of our forces in foreign land on patrol or fighting for some foreign nations, the shock to us would be enormous. We may not be able to recover from a blow so powerful.

Our greatest strength is our air power. How would we be able to apply it to defend ourselves? Drop bombs on our own citizens? Our strength would be greatly compromised.

Plus, how well would our forces overseas in foreign nations survive, when the strength of our nation at home is in turmoil? We are becoming a weakened nation.

Will we receive the same aid that we have been giving to nations around the world, since the end of World War II, if we start to fall? I doubt it.

Only a few may, but most nations, even after we've helped them for so long, don't like us. If the terrorists can keep us fighting in their backyard, the larger their forces can grow in our front yard. The United States may lose this war in the long run.

I believe that the terrorists could have cells throughout the country, waiting for this to happen. But I want to make clear that it is only speculation and nothing more.

The deep concern that I have and America should have also, is the rise of socialism in the United states. If this happens, and I am sure it will if we do nothing to stop it, then nothing else will matter.

I believe that it may be time for us to bring our troops home. Stop and think about it. I understand that we still have troops in Italy, Germany, France,

Japan, South Korea and many more nations as occupational forces.

Congressman Ron Paul claims we have troops stationed in 130 countries around the world. Why! For what purpose, and how many troops do we have throughout the world?

According to the Pentagon's most recent figures, the United States has around this globe, a little over one million service related personnel.

Broken down it appears like this. In active duty, on land, there are 448,743 personnel. At sea, on US Naval Vessels, there are 82,501. Combined, there is total of 531,244 men and women in service for our country throughout this world. We can add to that, 87,049 Defense department employee's. Also, we must add family, 396,122 spouses and children. This would total, 1,014,415 American's, serving our country, on foreign soil.

I will not attempt to list the amount of money we spend a year in all areas of the world. It has to be considerable. The United States has had service personnel in Europe and Japan for the last 70 or more years. Personnel serving in the rest of the world, over that many years, is hard for me to calculate, for the lack of information I have available, but the cost to our tax payers must be enormous.

Are there any reports of benefits received, related to the amounts of dollars spent? Can anyone imagine, how much was spent, just on keeping our presence in foreign lands around this world.

We have 1,014 415 people in the employ of our government spending their earning in foreign countries across the sea's. A good portion of that million plus people have been doing this for about 70 years.

Personnel and families that spend their salaries in the land they live in, that benefits the government and people of the land that they occupy.

It boggles the mind to even try to consider the amount of money spent on personnel needs. I cannot imagine what it has cost the American tax payer, over the many years of our presence on foreign land. We should bring all of our personnel, that are on foreign land home, and start using this force to protect our borders.

I believe that very soon we will be in a war for our existence as a nation. Not with Isis, or any terrorist groups, but with the progressives among us, that I wrote so much about earlier.

I strongly support the wall that Donald Trump wants to build. It is part of what we need and I do believe him when he said that Mexico will pay for it. Stopping illegal entrance into our land should be encouraged. So why has our government not taken any steps to do so? But to hinder what is good for our nation, once again, becomes the "Norm" by this administration.

We must start to close our borders, but more importantly, we need to dismantle this enemy within - the Fabian Society's Progressive Democrat's, as President Obama and Hillary Clinton have claimed themselves to be.

Americans are in battle on three fronts. The biggest battle is the progressive's, with and in tune with, the Fabian Society. They have formed so many powerful organizations, under a multitude of names.

Plus, the strong labor unions and the super powerful school unions, that have a deep influence over the democratic Senate and Congress through lobbying, with huge donations over the years, have enabled them to control the Democratic vote, to buy laws that favored their causes. It is as though the unions were on the floor of our senate voting themselves.

Second is the Jihad and Isis. The Democrat's stutter when they try to say their names. Stupid decisions were made in Iraq, pulling our troops out at a critical time, because President Obama wanted to declare the war was over under his watch.

This was strictly a political move, not caring at all, for the many Iraqi's lives that would be lost. Iraqi women and children, wounded and killed, now running for their lives, and happening in neighboring countries too. Also, the shameful beheading of our allies, their prisoners by Isis.

All of this so they could say Osama bin Laden is dead and our enemy is on the run. Just to win an election, to have 4 more years, to bring down this country from within.

Let's defend our cities, put our troops on our borders, and let's stop worrying about having occupational troops on foreign soil. Let us not lose our freedom. If we do, the world would then really suffer. I have said it earlier, I believe that if we lose our freedom, there will be no place in the world that freedom will ever exist again. Once freedom is lost, it will be gone forever.

We are fighting in a terrible war, not against a nation, but against a religious ideology, half a world away. Also at home, where our enemy, the progressive Fabian society, is at our door step.

This threat from the Fabian Society is much more of a danger to the existence of us, as a nation, than any war that we have been engaged in, ever in our history, since the war that we were in for our Independence on July 4th 1776, from the British.

Both the Jihads and the Fabian Society, independently feel that success is possible, only if they can destroy the nation that is in control of the free world, which is the United States of America.

Freedom for all the people is not their quest. The Jihads to have dominant male rule over all of us, is what they seek. Seeing how they treat their woman, is very sad.

Isis does not have to be a threat to the United States. The war that they brought to us can easily be won, if our current president, brought the necessary force, that we do have available, to fight them. We would have no problem to defeat them, if we brought the fight to them.

This is a war that we are in and we must treat it as a war. Mention them for what they are, Jihads', terrorists, but the President and his followers never do, for political reasons.

Our President thinks he can make the people believe, that he has stopped the war with the terrorists, which he did not. That the American people will believe him if he doesn't mention their name, but they do not.

He knows better, I am sure, but it is a tactic used by communists quite often. It is alright to lie, deny, not ever do you admit to wrong doing. Any deceitful thing you do is alright, as long as it serves their cause to benefit the socialist or communistic state.

The true reason, I believe, why he will not say Jihad terrorists is because he wants us to believe that they do not exist.

This threat must be considered by our government. Our borders must be secure. It was in 1993, that the World Trade Center, in New York City, was first attacked.

It is not inconceivable that thousands of terrorists have entered this country. Only since September 11, 2001, has our surveillance been greatly improved. However, the surveillance of our borders is still poor. Many illegal immigrants cross our borders even today and every day.

Terrorists have been fighting a war with us for the past 30 years, and amazingly, our government did not seem to be aware of "the gravity of it", until they took down the World Trade Center on September 11, 2001, with our own planes.

In 1983, terrorists took down our Marine barracks in Beirut, killing 241 Marines.

In 2000, they bombed the USS Cole in Aden, Yemen, killing 17 sailors and wounding 39.

On September 11, 2001, terrorists used four of our own airliners, to attack various targets in the USA, killing almost 3,000 people.

In 2002, I think the reality hit and we started to fight back. It took us 19 years to do something, only after we suffered a great deal of property damage, in the hundreds of billions of dollars, with 3,258 service members, and civilians killed and wounded, numbering in the hundreds.

I feel that this government should be paying more attention to what is happening, secure our borders, close them completely, and get some good immigration laws on the books. I cannot understand why they will not secure our borders.

A lot of promises are made, but nothing is ever done. I cannot see that it would be so difficult to do, or any reason why we would not want to, unless there is something going on that we should know.

It is so important for the hope of this world that the United States of America remains strong with proper leadership, in order to survive as a free nation. There is no other nation ever, that wanted for their people, freedom. The type of true freedom, that has been given to us, American's, by our forefathers.

It is frightening, having to realize the truth that is facing us. This nation, is in a planned takeover by an enemy, whose goal is to remake our country into socialist nation. They have already skillfully entwined themselves into the very fabric of which this nation is made of.

They have for many decades now, with great success, torn apart our Constitution, that laid open the possibility for this change to take place. I feel strongly that if one more president is elected that embraces the views of the present administration, America would then have moved so far to the left, that a changeover to socialism is then eminent. It is only a matter of time.

The oppressed people of the world, know better than the born citizens of America, the priceless value of our freedom. The United States is the only country, worldwide, where the people of most nations want to live.

I've often wondered why, when we fought to save the many nations of Europe and other parts of the world - Why! We did not introduce them to live under rules or laws of the United States. Laws that American citizens have been living with successfully for the last 240 years.

To do so we would have been justified, especially in Japan, Germany, Italy and Iraq, where they were our enemies that we defeated. I would believe that it would have made a big difference in this world if nations were to adopt our Constitution and our Bill of Rights, nations that we defeated. If they were the victor's, they would have taken complete control of the nations that fought against them, I am sure.

Imagine if we, the United States, insisted that these nations adopted our Constitution and Bill of Rights to become the laws of their land, as it would have been in our right to do. It would, I believe, have started a trend towards the freedom for nations of this world to see and want for their people.

A chance at freedom, that the people of these concurred countries would embrace. It, in my opinion, could have resulted in many nation's coming to realize how valuable and prosperous true freedom could be for their citizens.

It could have been the beginning of global peace for our world. That would have an honest approach to true freedom to the credit of these United States.

The oppressed people that are forced to live in the grip of socialism, would truly know how valuable this transformation to liberty could be.

So here we are, a nation under siege. This great nation may soon fall under the Fabian Society's ugly rule of socialism, because the danger that we are facing may not be realized in time.

American's - it is time for us to open our eyes. We must elect a man to become our President, that is proud of our country, courageous enough to fight for what is right for our country. We are a proud nation. Proven by our willingness to support the down trodden of this world.

We abound with generosity to the needy and are the supporters of freedom throughout the world. We are proud people living in a proud nation. We have been an inspiration to people throughout the world since our birth as a nation. We have no cause to bow to anyone ever.

We need a man in our White House, a man that has the strength and the willingness to want this, our country, to become great, once again. We must survive the evil of what the left is attempting to do. The nation we were a 100 years ago must be brought back.

Only if we, the United States of America, would realize the danger that we are facing, can we then stop this movement. A movement that has been slow and relentlessly driving this country to the left, with great success, for the last 90 or more years.

It appears to me, to be so strange, there is so much talk about winning wars, that we are fighting in lands so far away. There is no doubt that they are our enemies.

An enemy that is seeking to destroy the United States. An enemy that wants to bring their Religious ideology to all nations that make up this world that we live in.

We can, with the right leader in charge of our country, and the support of our allies that are also threatened. If well organized, we would have no trouble in defeating this enemy.

If we improve all aspects of our economy to become number one in the world. If we lead the world in advanced technology, in industry and also science. If our stock market reaches new heights never realized before.

Will these achievements make the United States of America great again?

If we are at war with two enemies on two different fronts and we defeat one of them, the one that we can physically see, can we really consider ourselves safe?

The truth is, we are at war with an enemy, that we are able to see, for a little more than a decade.

Also we are at war with an enemy, that has been invisible to us for more than nine decades.

Unless our leaders believe that this is happening, that this enemy is real and does exist, an enemy that has been secretly fighting us in our courts and picking away at our Constitution the many years that it has, if we cannot believe this is taking place, we will lose our freedom forever.

Then, America will never be able to become great, ever again. We will have lost this crucial battle. The freedom that was ours, will be transformed into socialism. Our Constitution, our Bill of Rights will be torn to shreds. Over many decades later, that will pass, the knowledge that America, at one time, was a free nation, will not be believed.

In most of our public schools today, American history is already being distorted, because of the strength of the progressive movement and unions, already having a controlling effect on our Board of Education.

Our history books and lessons of America's greatness will be removed and never taught in the classrooms of America again. As time moves on, there will be no records of our existence at all.

Let us not kid ourselves, can we consider that we are free under the rule of socialism? Will it matter who our friends are, if we are under the control of our enemy and no longer citizens of a free nation?

All the rights that were ours will be lost forever, replaced with fear of the leadership that took control of the country that once belonged to the people. Never again will there be a voice to be heard from anyone. We will become silenced and oppressed by the authority that now controls us.

There will not be a Democratic or Republican party to do battle with each other, having honest discussions about laws that will best benefit the will of the citizens of this once great nation. We will all belong to one party, the socialist party, like it or else.

Our quality of living will slowly be reduced to one step above slavery. Earnings will be limited, no longer will there be a tolerance for any complaints a person may have.

All people, the many millions of citizens of this once great nation, will be working for the government. We will have lost our will to compete. Skills will have diminished, striving for equality is made simple.

Everyone will be poor, except for the upper class, where from the fruits of the labor of the poor, they will become very wealthy.

Our health care system will become a disaster for sure. Imagine yourself being treated in a hospital in Cuba. That is if you can secure a bed before it becomes too late.

Let's think about our recent scandals, now happening with the Veterans hospitals throughout our country. Men and women that have put their lives on the line, at a moment's notice, now waiting months to see a doctor for needed help. Is this the responsibility of our present administration?

This will become the norm for the millions of our citizens in need of medical attention in our once great free nation, America. Our health care system, being one of the best ever in the world, will be reduced to what it will become, in nations under socialist control.

Part 3

DRUGS AND THE COST TO THE USA

We also have a serious drug problem in the states and cities across, the United States of America, for far too long. It has been a long term problem for 10% of people on drugs and 20% of our citizens, that must live and deal with the addicted.

The tragedy is when children, 12 years of age and older, into their teens, become addicted, which happens quite often to the youth of America.

This tragedy compounds itself, a million fold, to a family, when it's your son or daughter that is the victim of this horrendous addiction. I do not believe that a 12-year-old child expresses a willingness to get themselves hooked on crack cocaine or any other kind of drug.

Children, at the early age of 9, have become addicts, but I believe not through a desire of their own. There is always someone out there, ready to take advantage of their vulnerability. Drugs have an effect on 30% of our citizens.

It is sad but true, that there are villainous people in our society, who feel no guilt in selling drugs to minors. Their gain is the hope, that they have created another addict, to become a source of money, for years to come. For the children and their families, it becomes an endless nightmare, which could, and many times does, end in death.

There are many points of view discussed about legalizing the use of drugs. There are strong arguments that are expressed on both sides of this issue. One argument I hear quite often is, if drugs are legalized, half the teenagers in America would become addicted. Overdosing would become a huge problem for teens and grown-ups alike.

I totally disagree with that concept. I believe that the complete opposite would happen. Most that become addicted are usually talked into taking their first hit. It is not likely that children who are age 9 or 12, would just decide one day to venture out seeking to become high.

More likely, they have a friend that is a user that is talking them into trying drugs the first time. Once tried, it does not take much to become hooked on drugs, especially with crack cocaine.

I strongly oppose our drug laws for many reasons. Prisons were built to keep criminals off of our city streets. Less than 50% of the inmates in our prisons are there for reasons other than drug related crimes. More than 50% are in prison with drug related crimes and have a criminal record that shouldn't be theirs.

Drug users are not criminals, they are addicts. This percentage varies from year to year. More than 50% of prisoners that are in our jails, are there because of the war on drugs. This war has been going on for more than hundred years. In the year of 2014 we had close to 99,000 prisoners in our jails due to drug related crimes.

Imagine if we didn't legalize alcohol during the probation era of the 20's, how many more addicts would be occupying our jails today. It would almost be doubled. However, they too are not criminals, they are addicts. It must be seen for what it is, it's an illness.

They should be and are today, handled as addicts. I feel the same should be the case with the drug addicted citizens of our country. Do not burden them with criminal behavior, because it is an illness, as are alcoholics.

If alcohol addiction was considered a crime, liquor would become scarce. The price would triple or quadruple from what it should be, immediately.

You would see little difference in the behavior of an alcoholic or that of a hard drug user, and the crime rate of alcoholics would rise.

The extreme heartache and pain to them and their families, also would rise, due to being unfairly incarcerated, as the drug addicts are today.

Take into consideration that the war on drugs started more than a hundred years ago. A lot has changed since then. Our population, when this war on drugs began, was approximately 83 million people. We are now at 321 million people.

Science and medical knowledge over the last 100 years has advanced considerably. When that war began, they were raiding drug dens and not much more.

It was not the huge business that it is today. A lot of issues are different. There is now four times as many people. Drug pushers are out there influencing our children, developing future customers. We must stop all of this, we must stop the crime involved and the pain to user and family.

The only way to stop the crime's that are married to drugs, is to not make it a crime, legalize the drugs.

There are so many advantages in doing this. Think about the relief to mothers and fathers, to wives or husbands and children and the addict themselves.

The long years of anguish would finely be over.

We can put some experienced minds to work. We could find many solutions to this problem, besides helping all the people affected by our drug situation. We, as a nation, can save billions of dollars yearly.

A news person that I listen to at 8 PM, on a regular basis, is firmly against the legalization of drugs. He has on several occasions said to legalize drugs would only cause more people to become drug addicts.

As much as I respect this man, I feel that he is dead wrong. I believe he has not had first-hand experience of what happens in the life of a drug addicted person and the tremendous hurt that is brought to the entire family of the person that is addicted.

This gentleman has control of the mike. His messages reach a large audience. If he could give a more, Fair and Balanced thought to this serious problem, it would mean a lot to the suffering taking place across our country.

In the homes of the addicted, the pain and hardship brought to their families is pitiful. The many that are involved that suffer, from one person's addiction is huge.

Try to realize that the users are trapped in the hell of their addiction. Instead of giving them help to escape the hell that they are in, we do the opposite. We straddle them with a record of criminal charges and throw them in jail.

Realize that addicts are human beings that have been caught in a web that has entangled their lives. Not being able to ever escape this hell they are in, placed there because of the greed of someone that profits from the pain of others, the addicted living in the hope, that one day, they too can be freed.

I can only hope that I can get someone with influence to read what I have to say. His great influence, because of his status on TV, is powerful. I would like to see him opine in favor of legalizing drugs.

We must begin to realize what pressure the addict is put through to satisfy his addiction. The pain is twofold for the parents, to see the helpless suffering that their child is going through with having this continuous haunting desire, masked in the fear that they will not be able to afford their next fix, which remains as the controlling factor in the behavior of the addicted.

Try to understand the pressure put upon them, to assist them in having the means to acquire the drugs that their child needs, knowing of the upheaval that will take place in their home, if their needs are not satisfied.

Reluctantly, you give him the money to help him get through another day. Sometimes it leaves you without money that you needed for your wife and yourself.

It is so hard to say no, knowing that if he does not have his fix, it will only result in more suffering for your child, that you know, you do not have the means or ability to cure.

But it is your child that was introduced to marijuana at the very young age of nine, that you were not aware of until recently. Now he has become a grown young man using crack cocaine, with a never ending problem.

He is addicted, it becoming more severe with each passing day. A burden that has become so deeply rooted into your life. There is no relief in sight, for the demand for drugs on your child is never ending. The fear of pain, when going into withdrawal, is constantly on their mind.

His problem worsens as time goes by, he now wanders the streets and is away from home for days.

You try not to think, that the worse might be happening to him. Your mind can never rest, in the state of mind that he is always in, is very frightening to you and your wife.

Actually you are glad to see him, when after a few days he comes home, because you can see that he is not hurt in any way, but the lingering drug problem is always there. He will say he is hungry and you feed him, then the demand for money begins.

For many years this has been going on. It is a very painful situation that seems to be never ending. You feel there is nothing more you can do to help him. You have heard of tough love, can that be an answer, as you have heard it may be?

It is about 10:30 at night and there is a knock at your door. It can be no one else but your son. Is this the time to practice tough love, that you hear talked about so much? It becomes the most difficult approach to take, having tried it myself to do for the first time.

If you want to know the feeling of a broken heart, bring yourself to turning your child away, knowing in your heart that he needs you the most.

There he stands before you, your loving child in pain, asking to come in, but you have decided on tough love. You have taken the first step, you have to be firm, all that you have tried before has not worked.

You pray to yourself that this may well have good results. You continue to refuse him. It was a drizzly chilly night he has just a thin jacket on, his face looks tired and is dirty, as are the rest of his cloths.

With a lump in your throat and tears in your eyes, the answer is still no. He turns and walks away, as he walks down the path away from your home. You open your door and try to yell to come back, but you can't get the words out because you are too choked up to speak.

You remain with a blurred image of him as he walks out of sight. You never expect the pain of that moment to ever leave you or your wife, his mother, and it never does. Once he's left, you have no way of knowing where he would go or be.

Unless you have lived through having a son or daughter that is going through this suffering from being addicted, it is hard to understand the pain and suffering a family is put through.

I knew for sure that my son would do anything to be free of his addiction. The life he is in is not one he chose for himself, it is one that was chosen for him. I am not alone, this series of events has been happening many times over, in many homes across America.

This is what so many people do not understand, most addicts are actually tricked into becoming

addicted. This is the way the drug business works.
They can only make money if there is someone out
there to sell to. Their whole business relies on
them having people that are addicts.

Pushers have become very skilled at creating them.
It is so easy for a pusher to take control of a young
innocent mind.

We have been fighting this drug war for over a
hundred years, without any apparent improvement,
with an enormous amount of money being spent. It
might be that legalizing drugs could turn this
problem around.

We would see less people on drugs, if drugs were
legalized, because I would imagine that children,
12 years of age and younger, would not know much
about drugs as they do today.

There would not be someone encouraging the
young innocent minds of our children to try drugs.
There is an average of close to 8,000 people turned
on to drugs each day, 54% are under 18 years of
age.

I believe that any child that was not encouraged to
try crack cocaine, or any other of the drugs, would
not on their own seek a way to obtain drugs at all.
It would just not be in their interest to do so.

This alone would cause an amazing drop in the percentage of addicts that would be on the streets in our neighborhoods. It would be a great day for our youth and their family's all across America.

Think of the advantages of being rid of the pushers of drugs, and the effect it would have on our communities. It would stop some crimes overnight.

Drug cartels would be out of business on our borders and throughout the United State of America for good.

The crimes of pick pockets and mugging committed mostly by drug addicts, giving them the quick cash that they need to be spent on drugs would greatly be reduced, making our streets safer.

Businesses being robbed at gun point, homes being broken into at all hours of the day and night, would also be reduced by a large percentage. America will become a safer place. It will start to appear more like the American dream that it once was.

When our country is a safer place to live, the cost of policing our country would decrease, reducing the cost to our tax payers. Money would be saved in many areas of local and state governments. It is difficult for me to estimate how huge the amount of saving would be, but it would be extremely high.

Our country can make this happen, and we should, for the safety of the general public, the reduced cost of incarceration, the aid given to the addicts, and for the relief their families would have.

The inmates that are in jail for drug use or for drug related crimes, make up more than half the population, by about 20,000 inmates yearly. Presently, we have close to 99,000 inmates jailed, strictly on drug related crimes throughout the United States, at a cost of approximately $44,000 a year, per inmate. This totals to be approximately $4,336,376,000 a year.

These numbers only reflect the cost of incarceration. Consider all the other costs involved. Our streets being safer, requiring less law enforcers, our court systems with fewer cases to deal with, and our prisons would need less guards having greatly reduced the number of prisoners.

Less jail space would be required, we would save on the cost of building jails and their up-keep. To say that the legalization of drugs is foolish or that it would make our situation worse, is not true.

The cost per inmate in New Jersey, is $44,000, in California it is over $48,000, and in some states it is as high as $60,000 a year per inmate. Having to maintain a staff large enough to handle the inmates and all the above mentioned, is only a part of the savings.

The additional cost of drug addicts to their families, that is constant, must also be considered. Seek out people that you may know, friends or relatives in your family, with a drug problem in their home. What is the cost to them? This has also been part of the cost of our war on drugs, that has been going on for 100 years or more.

The amount of money spent over the many years of this ongoing battle on drugs, could result in unbelievable savings, if drugs are decriminalized.

We can take control of this bad situation, and make better use of the monies saved, to help the addicted of our country, if we would stop this ongoing unnecessary war on drugs.

Factual numbers put together in the early part of 2014, showed that there was a total of 176,858 inmates, in correctional facilities throughout the United States.

The total that was related to drug crimes of this number, was approximately 98,500 inmates. This would mean that all other crimes, any imaginable crime you can think of combined, would have been committed by a total of the remaining 78,000 inmates.

Amazingly if drugs were legalized, more than half that are in jail now, could possibly be placed on parole or be released. I would put a committee together that would analyze every case, before releasing them.

Aid to 10% of our citizens on drugs, could then be had for them, starting programs to release them from their addictions, and paid for with the monies saved from jailing them. In my opinion, jailing them is definitely not the answer.

To understand this tragic chain of events, you must able to imagine living with the constant hardship that has been brought to bear on the families and the victims of being addicted. The destructive behavior that comes with addiction, sadly affects every member of a family.

The change in lifestyle and loyalty to love ones, quickly in the mind of an addict disappears. A need to satisfy a drug habit, dominates their thought process. Where will they get enough money for their next fix?

This comes to the front of their mind, the moment they awake. It remains with them, till they are able to buy a fix. A never ending cycle forms and continues to plague them for days, months, or even years on end.

It is a very sad happening in the lives of so many young men and women. This is not a life they chose for themselves, it is the life dealt to them by the evil that lives among us.

There is never enough money for them to satisfy their drug problem, justifying their concerns, their fears, of not being able to afford another fix.

Think about what they are forced to go through. It is not the pleasure that they may receive from having drugs in their system, that drives them. It is the agony of their body wroth with pain, reminding them of what lies ahead, knowing they are sure to suffer if they cannot avail themselves of the drugs their body requires.

When we wittiness the behavior of an addict in their quest for drugs, we see them as selfish, wanting others to support a habit that is for their pleasure. We seldom realize what is really taking place, that they are fearful of the pain that withdrawal will bring to them. It is a sad and helpless situation that they are dealing with.

They exhaust the one's they love, asking for the help they want, never for the help they need because they know the pain of withdrawal, having been on the edge of agony, when their system starts to become void of drugs.

You can tell in their eyes, the duel pain they feel, the one in their gut and the hurt that their family is made to suffer, as a result of their addiction. The pressure put on loved ones is relentless, usually ending up in a guilty rage, angered because of their desperate need for a fix, which often does not end well.

Resulting suffering from their behavior, becomes secondary for the need to obtain their next fix, is always first on the minds of an addict.

The sad truth is that they can do nothing to ease the pain that they brought to their family, but it does add to their suffering, of being addicted, knowing how much their addiction has depressed themselves and the ones they love.

They usually turn away from their family as a result of a sober moment, when the reality of their situation surfaces.

The haunting truth of their disruptive behavior, coupled with the taunting need to escape into what most believe is their fantasy world, and that, is not the case at all. It only adds to the terrible dilemma active in their mind.

As the effects of the drugs wear off, the sad reality of their situation begins to surface once again. It becomes impossible for the addicted to deal with curing themselves of their addiction.

Try to imagine the confused state that their mind is in, when stressed to the point of despair if a fix is not available to them. It truly is an awful state of mind to be in.

They become distraught, they have lost the respect of friends, they are too ashamed to approach family, because of the unfair demands they have asked of them, but regardless of their behavior, they are the ones that continue to suffer. They must live with the ever presence of their need, to have the next fix, which never leaves them.

There is no one there to share their grief. They have no one left to turn to, yet the relentless demand for drugs remains. The only relief for their drugged worn body is to have their dose of drugs.

The more drugs that are fed into their system, the more their body will demand. It becomes an endless struggle with no relief to be had. They become void of reasoning, nothing said can reach them, words they have heard so many times before from loved ones, cannot erase the worry of not having their next fix.

Can we really feel their pain? The empathy is not there. We are not alive in the mind of a drug addict, because we have not lived as they have, placed where they are unknowingly, by the evil that thrives on the unfortunate soles that they have become.

How many men and women, that have lived the life of a drug addict will read this? Not many, because they probably will be gone. They have for the longest time, lost control of their lives. To obtain enough money for the next fix never leaves.

They have no dreams of a better life, there is no pleasant thoughts for them, to live in a normal lifestyle as in a world they may have at one time known. They do not ever see themselves as having a future.

They have a loss of interest in all things, except how will they get the money to satisfy their habit. It becomes the only thoughts in the drug users mind. The feeling they have of the embarrassment of what they have become, is always with them.

But how can they change, how can they begin to make their lives normal once again? Most of the money that they acquired, if any, will be spent on drugs. Very little is ever spent on nourishment.

Weight loss is readily apparent as to the depth of their addiction, and the toll that drugs have taken on their bodies, and eventually their life, will always be there.

They must learn to live with rejection. It is what they get on a daily basis, constantly asking for help. It only adds to their depression of knowing there is no escape from the tormented mind which is theirs.

They, frighten and confused, plagued with that feeling of emptiness that enters the minds of the lonely, can only be felt by, or understood, by druggies that are caught and faced with the same predicament.

It becomes a desperate situation. A drug weakened mind enters into a new phase of their saddened life. The avenues they once had open to obtain drugs, have closed. Their choices are few and has now been reduced, to them committing crimes.

They really have no choices. It has become a do or die situation for them. To find a job, to work? In the many attempts made, they could not get through the eight-hour day. Work is out of the question. Their span of concentration is just not there.

The reality of their situation must be realized, that they are in a fight for their life. They are not hardened criminals, they are confused human beings, their body is demanding its supply of drugs, they know that when that growling in their stomach begins, it will lead to the excruciating pain of possible withdrawal.

There were several times when the absence of drugs causes the beginning of withdrawal. Fear and desperation takes over, knowing the pending punishment their body may have to endure. If a supply of drugs is not available, the pain in their gut is sure to return as a reminder. What is left for them to do?

Rehab is very expensive, and in most cases they or their family cannot afford it. Even if, somehow they could get rehabilitation, the first thing that they would have to face, would be withdrawal.

Worn out from the ordeals they have suffered up until now, how could they go through that pain once more, besides their being so depressed as they are at that moment.

Their suffering is almost never-ending, understood or realized, yet all surrounding life moves on. Their life remains stagnant, penniless and frightened of what lies ahead, and weighs heavy on their minds. It is at this time that their awkward approach to crime usually begins.

In most cases it is short lived for many reasons, but mainly due to a lack of experience, because I estimate, that about ninety-five percent of drug addicts, do not have a criminal mind.

They have nowhere to turn and will do anything in desperation to get out of the sickening situation they find themselves in.

However, they have committed a crime, and according to the severity of the offense, they will serve time in jail. It is a terrible moment for them. They are frightened, nervous without representation, and very few of them could ever afford a lawyer, and so they must rely on a court assigned attorney.

This becomes a major change in their lives. In jail, with only slight medical assistance, they will go through withdrawal once more.

Now among thousands of inmates, they are feeling alone. But they begin to realize that being incarcerated, can have some advantages. They are over their withdrawal, and are getting three meals a day.

Along with gaining weight and body strength, the relationship with family is there once again and most importantly, they are off drugs. That long lasting painful nightmare is over.

Besides the abuses that prisons can bring, a new and better life can emerge from the hell that it was, to what it could now become. It is sad to look back - their past will never leave them now. They are sober now, though their regrets are many and haunting. The reality is, there is a new chance now at living a normal life.

Relations with their family is also greatly improved, as much as it hurts to have your child in jail, their families can breathe a sigh of relief. They are no longer roaming the streets, coming and going all hours of the day and night.

Their parents can now believe that their son is free of drugs and out of harm's way. It permits them to feel relaxed and to be free of worry, for the first time in more than a decade.

After a very long time, life returns to normal for them. Both parents have now reached retirement age, looking for that comfortable change that retirement can bring.

Their hope is that when their son comes home from jail, the events that brought him there are over, and as a drug free man, he will find a job and start to live a normal life.

That he will become a visitor to their home, not the ill-behaved, fighting, and demanding person he had become and remained to be for many long years.

After many years of unnecessary suffering, and all the pain and suffering caused to friends and family, was all because of one scoundrel, who had decided that your son or daughter would be one of many, that had been persuaded into becoming a user of drugs, to enrich this pusher's life.

So many years as a drug user has taken its toll. Now much older, home and with love ones, away from the pressure of how jail can impact a person's life, is over.

You are ready to start anew. Naturally you must find work in order to get started in what you want to have, a new and better life. You start to feel good about yourself for a change.

All the wasted years spent on drugs, along with time in jail, has left you without skills or the ability to qualify for a decent paying job. It is a serious setback, but the effort to find work continues.

When applying for work, there is on most applications, that one question - have you ever been incarcerated? It is something you had never expected to see, or thought you would ever have to deal with, is the time that you spent in jail.

Again and again, you are faced with that one question, with every form for work you attempt to file. How do you answer that one question?

The whole chain of events that brought you to where you are, tells you that your past will never let you be free. How can you gain the trust of one, who in reality is a stranger to you, to place you in their employ? Why should they take a chance with you, when there are many others with clean records available?

Your jail time will become a huge factor in most cases to secure a decent lifestyle. There is no understanding from anyone, outside of your family, to what took place in your life. How drugs have played a major part in crippling every move you try to make to better yourself.

That at a very young and innocent age, against your knowledge of it, you became addicted to drugs. This, all because you were befriended and talked into, what was to become a living nightmare, by a friend that was already hooked on drugs, or by a drug dealer in your neighborhood.

You now are faced with reality, that there is very little chance of ever landing a decent job. You are now much older, alone and relying on your parents for support. A very depressing place to be.

Self-pity starts to warp their thinking and the exposure to drugs is always there. The reality he is facing, is that he believes he has no future.

He is older and wiser now, he knows that he could handle being high, and stop whenever he wants. Besides, he has suffered enough and deserves the relaxing feeling that a little bit of pot will give him.

Sad to realize but the nightmare starts all over again. It did not take more than one week to be hooked again on crack cocaine and once more the horrors of drugs started to take its toll on him and his family again.

This series of the above events are true, he, my son Steven, was brutally murdered on July 10, 2008, because he owed a 21-year-old drug pusher, $126 dollars. That young black man killed my son.

He Killed my son Steve, because he wanted to impress members of a drug cartel that he wanted to become a member of. He had to show he was tough enough to take another man's life.

He was murdered, early in the morning of July 10, 2008, on a road east of the Pocono race track in Pennsylvania. The crime scene indicated that more than one person was involved in his murder, but this young man never admitted to that.

I will not go into the details of this crime, only to say that the money that my son owed, was to justify this awful crime. The reason this young man did what he did, in my opinion, was to prove that he was capable of murder. It was so brutal and so cruel a murder that his body could not be displayed.

Murdered my son to gain entry into a gang of criminals. Now this is the thought pattern of a cold blooded killer, this is a young man that has a criminal mind. He received a sentence of 16 years to 40 years. With good behavior he can be free within 16 years.

My son did not have a criminal mind - he was not a criminal.

He was a poor unfortunate sole that became hooked on drugs at a very young age, through no fault of his own. He never had a chance to develop into a normal educated young man.

This, his murder and all the sad events that happened in my son's life could have been different, if only he could have found a decent job when he came out of jail the first time.

Finding a job, would mean he would be alive today, but he was labeled a criminal because of the war on drugs.

The pain to him and the suffering to the ones that loved him, all could have been avoided, if using drugs was legalized.

Just to be able to say NO, to that one question. "Have you ever been incarcerated?", would have made a big difference in how his future could have changed for the better.

If we can convince our government to make drugs legal, because it should be considered an illness not a crime, it would be an important step in assisting the largest group of ill people, in our nation, that are addicted.

According to CBS News, there is close to 10% of our population that use illegal drugs, which amounts to approximately 32 million, age 12 and older, in the United States, that are on illegal drugs.

People turn to using drugs in our country, on average of 7,800 per day. More than half, 54.1%, are under the age of 18. Usually, they are members of the poorer families in our society, or are on public assistance programs.

Being from a poor family, increases the burden of the user and their entire family. Not being able to afford drugs is what develops into criminal behavior. Very few of the wealthy, have a problem getting drugs, or suffer the effects of drugs.

If they do, they usually have a good hospital plan for the treatment they may need. Poor people are afraid that they would be admitting that they are using illegal drugs if they seek medical help, and would possibly end up in jail.

This would not be the case if drugs were legalized. We are supposed to be living in a nation that is free. That should give a person the right to do what they want to do, if their actions do not bring harm to others. Isn't that what it is all about? Either we are a free nation or we are not.

If anyone, drug user or not, if their behavior is not causing harm to anyone and also are not breaking the law in any way, wouldn't it become their right, if they are not being unlawful, and are of age, to take their life into their own hands?

We automatically assume, that the addict is going to hurt somebody. That normally would never happen, but only does, because drugs are illegal. That is always the reason why crimes are committed by them. Their urgent need for some illegal drugs is always the only reason they commit crimes.

In my opinion, we should legalize drugs. We should reduce the cost of marijuana, making it affordable for users. It should be taxed at a reasonable rate, so as to not encourage black markets to form again.

This would get rid of drug cartels, pushers and the

black market in our country, overnight. Corruption and our crime rates that were related to drugs would end. Billions of dollars would be saved.

Most importantly, we must never forget that drugs are a health issue. Rehabilitation should always be encouraged, and also be available to the addicted, with the offer of painless detoxing.

Helping them, I feel, is the responsibility of our government. They became illegal drug users because of our laws, which also labeled them as criminals, and they were not. If drugs were made legal, the criminal burden would be removed.

They, in most cases, were tricked into the use of drugs at a very innocent age, forcing them into very hard times for most of their lives. The law compounded their pain, making them criminals and punished them, instead of helping them, as they should have.

Our government put them in jail, a terrible place for them to be. Consider the suffering they had endured over all of the year that they were addicted, because they were labeled illegal drug users. And they were not.

The suffering for them and their families was cruel and unjust, so painful, so very long lasting, and most of all, unnecessary and undeserving in the least.

It is easy to say that the addicts are criminals, that by using illegal drugs they have committed a crime. The real criminals, in my mind, are the people that continually force the addicts into the life of crime, by not legalizing drugs.

Also, they that live off of the suffering of the addicted and their families, not wanting to give up their lucrative jobs at the expense of the addicted.

Have them live a month, or a week, or even a day, in a house where a person on drugs resides. Then, imagine the suffering to their families, having to live there for years on end.

Why is it so difficult to legalize drugs? Drugs have grown into a business worth close to $35 billion dollars yearly, is this the reason why? A growing business that is legal, aside from the illegal sales of drugs itself. Why legalize drugs? Unionized trade's that are involved in jail building?

The guards needed, to watch over close to 99,000 inmates would be reduced to less than half or maybe all. If drugs are legalized, rehabilitation centers would lose customer's, because addicts, in some cases, were ordered by the Judicial system to become rehabilitated. Why give away all this money that is being made?

Courts will become less crowded. Fewer lawyers and court personnel and judges will be needed. Less law enforcement required to police our neighborhoods would be needed.

Some people in government, may or would lose their jobs as a direct result of the legalization of drugs. They have been profiting for decades from the pain and suffering of the addicts and their families.

All of them have been making a living on the misfortune of the addicted. Their work force size could slowly be reduced, I am sure. Isn't it about time that they give something back to these unfortunate human beaning?

Finland, a country that has legalized drugs for a long time now, show very little crime from their drug population. They have sectioned parts of their cities for drug user's to live, and are doing very well and their crime rate is still down.

The same with Portugal, their drug use has been legal for several years now and there has been hardly any change in the amount of drugs used since they have legalized drugs.

When did our government decide that drugs should be considered unlawful to use? Why didn't they leave alcohol use to be illegal, and have drugs use to be legal? What would be the difference?

There is no difference! We have over 12 million alcohol addicted people in the USA that are involved in various crimes. A high percentage are felon's and child beaters. Over 70% have been accused in both forms of criminal behavior.

Also, you can add to their criminal list, rape and wife battering. Alcoholism is responsible for over 70% of the stabbings and over 80% of homicides.

As a result of having family, women and their children in their home, the suffering to family, will add another 40 or 50 million to the list of people affected from the use of alcohol.

There is a $60-billion-dollar cost that is related to health care and social programs, and let us not forget drunken drivers who are having accidents that are caused by drinkers that have maimed and killed so many over the years.

Alcoholism is very expensive. So why is one illegal and the other is not? It just does not make sense.

Both should be legalized. Let's get the addicted the help they so urgently need. Let us ease the pressure placed on the mothers and fathers, also sibling that may be affected by that one person's addiction.

The United States has approximately 32 million drug addicts. It would mean that 32 million families throughout our country are forced to deal with a drug problem within their homes. It is so difficult to explain the suffering that is forced on that household, not just for years, but for decades.

In some cases, the grief and heartache is endless, and it involves everyone in your family. The hurt is not on the addicted alone but is suffered by the mother and father alike. If there is a sister or brother or both, they also see and are forced to endure the awful chain of events that unfolds, caused by someone that is addicted, living in that home.

Millions of people of all ages, in millions of homes across this nation, dealing with the anguish and worry for their child. As much as you are hurting from witnessing your child's pains, it is they, that are suffering the real pain of their addiction.

As much as you want to be of help, you know you cannot afford to help them. It really becomes a hopeless situation. A situation that doesn't have to be, if drugs were legalized.

On average, if we use a family of four as the

normal family size, it would amount to128 million people, or more than 1/3 of the population of American's that are caused to suffer because of the lack of understanding of this ongoing drug problem that we are having.

Our rehabilitation centers, all 14,000 of them, if they employed 20 people in each center, it would amount to 280,000 men and women in their employ.

Can we imagine how wrong this is? To keep 280,000 people happily employed, we are willing to sacrifice the lives of 128 million people. Is this the reason why we do nothing for the poor members of our country? Amazing! Will we ever be able to convince the people at the helm of this country to see the need to legalize drugs.

Our Congress and Senate are in this position now, to make these changes. Will we be able to vote in a president, with enough compassion, not only for the addicted but for the family of the addicted as well.

Try to understand the reality, of the many who are affected, by the one person in a family that is suffering from the terrible addiction.

We as a nation are faced with serious problems that need to be addressed. This great country should not be having a drug problem that is out of control because we are not making the proper effort. Changes that are needed are never made!

Are we willing to stand by and do nothing to help so many of our drug addicts who are in great need, not to disturb the lives of a few?

We are American's, or are we not? This is not the American way! We have traveled half way around the world to assist nations of people. We fought wars in their behalf to help them.

We did whatever we could, because we were able to realize their problems and willingly gave our support to them. We have spent billions of dollars in wars for them.

Well we are here now, in our home land. We have a serious problem, as we were able to realize the problems of other nations. I do hope someone will step up and realize the major problems, we, this once great nation of ours, is now facing.

My son was born on February 17, 1961. Today he would be 54 years old. He was murdered on July 10, 2008. He was 47 years old.

The hurt we feel, lives on in the household of thousands of families in America. Families who may have a son or daughter that are suffering from an addiction, as we were. I am certain that we are not alone. More than one third of America's 128 million people in our country, suffer one way or another, from drug related problems.

Had drugs been legalized before these events took place, my son, along with other addicted sons and daughters, that have died as a result of a drug overdose, or any other drug related reason, I am sure most would be alive today.

The presiding Judge had, through the detectives handling our sons case, asked that we, his family, write letters to court. I believe the purpose being, was to express to the court or jury, the loss that we were feeling and suffering of losing our son, especially under such painful circumstances.

My family proceeded to write letters in response to the judges' request. This is my Wife's letter to the court:

Dear Honorable Judge,   *10/28/2009*

I was asked to express my feelings to you about what loss I feel in losing my son. I find this very difficult to talk about. I loved my son deeply. Steven always showed a deep love for me and his family too. He was a good person and didn't deserve the fate that was dealt him by an uncaring despicable KILLER.

It was on July 10, 2008 when two strange, well dressed men, in dark suits, came walking up my walkway, to my front door. A funny feeling rose up inside of me. Something is not right I thought, but I never expected them to bring to me and my family, that horrible news of my son's death.

I had just spoken to him just the day before, early in the morning. He sounded 'up' and said that he was going to get help. He was addicted and was seeking help from the Penn Foundation.

He was assuring me that he would be OK again. He wanted to be a responsible human being. He had been going through hard times being addicted, and once again saw an opportunity to be well again.

He knew my husband and I worried so much about him. He was trying to relieve our pain and deep concern. So the news that the two detective's brought to us was even more shocking.

I didn't feel the, immediate reality, of what was being said. I refused to believe he was gone forever. For months afterwards, I still had the feeling that he would come walking through my front door.

That this was some kind of a bad dream or was just

not true. Or maybe they had the wrong guy here. It couldn't be my son!

My son is gone. I will never feel his touch or hear his voice again, while his killer might live on. Who can understand the bonding love a mother has for a child, regardless of what age they are? What right did anyone have to decide that I should suffer the loss of a son?

How can anyone take it on their own, to bring me to this nauseating suffering? I shall carry it in my heart till' my breaths are no more. They have sentenced me to suffer a lifetime of mental anguish.

There is no cure for the pain that I feel, there is nothing I can do but to deal with the anger that grows inside of me each day of my life.

My son was not a mean man. He would never knowingly bring harm to anyone. Steven was always ready to give a helping hand when asked.

The people that knew him loved him. He was a good man. He was addicted to drugs since he was nine years old. I never knew this. I only found out about his addiction, the first time he was incarcerated.

I don't know how to deal with the loss of my son. I hurt some days more than others. Night time is the worst time for me.

I don't sleep well anymore. Steven is always on my mind. I know that his murderer lives on and I am haunted by the thought of why. Why did this man decide that my son's life should end? What was my son thinking? What was the last moment of life for my son? Did he die instantly? Did he linger for a while, with the realization that his life would soon be over?

How painful were the moments before he died? How much did he suffer mentally?

Was he in captivity and being led to a place to be executed? If so, how long did he live knowing he was going to die? Was it hours, moments, how long was it? Was this the decision of one man, or were there others? Was it necessary to shoot him four times?

Did the first bullet kill him and the other three shots made in contempt, to show the disregard that this man has for another man's life? Did he have to find it necessary to run him over several times with his car?

I was not able to see my son in death, for this man mutilated his body so badly. How cruel can this murderer be? Will he one day be set free? With a mind like his, will he be in a position again to decide the fate of someone else's life, someone else's child, brother, husband, father, like he did my son's?

I pray that he is dealt with the same justice that he decided for my son, Steven. How can all of this have happened? Will I ever be free of these thoughts and feelings?

This criminal not only decided my son's fate, he also took a part of life from all the rest of the people that loved Steven, my husband, his sister, his two brothers, his son and niece's and all the people that knew and loved him. We shall never forget what this evil man did to us, what he took from us.

Your Honor, I don't envy your position. I know you have to make so many difficult but wise choices in cases like this. So my prayers and blessings are with you. I am confident you will make whatever decisions are proper, and I will respect whatever you decide is just.

Please just consider what this man has done to my family and myself, before you make your decision in this case. We are counting on you to do the right thing and we trust that you will.

Yours Truly,
Joan A. Santillo

There are so many reasons why we should legalize drugs.

Most see it as a lone person, guilty of a drug crime, that is standing before a Judge, being sentenced to jail. Little can be shown of what the truth is about that individuals' life, and how severely damaged a brain can become, from the pain and hell of their addiction. A tortured mind, desperately searching for a way to be relieved of the pending pain, that will come, if a fix is not available.

Try to imagine the amount of money spent and wasted, that incarcerating someone amounts to. And what benefit is there in spending all of this money? At $44,000 a year for a sentence of 5 years, will have cost the government, approximately $220,000. In some states more and some less.

The cost of sending them to forced rehabilitation by the court, would be considerably less than putting them in jail. To rehabilitate someone, treatment might vary from approximately 28 days to 120 days of rehabilitation.

With the proper treatment and follow through they will, or could become, free of drugs. If we decriminalize drugs, the effects of their treatment, I certainly believe, would in some cases, be an everlasting permanent cure for them.

There is no doubt in my mind that we can slowly remove the problem of drugs, that has been plaguing our society for almost a hundred years.

Imagine one hundred years of a fight with drugs, and we as a nation, have given so little thought to solve. Why?

Not only the suffering addicted, but also the heartache suffered by their parents and their siblings. The lingering torturous pain that a mother feels when a child is lost forever.

There is no end to the repercussions brought on by having drugs being illegal. I introduced the above letter by my wife, trying to show how far reaching and to what extent the drug problem is, and of keeping the use of drugs illegal.

The endless suffering and hurt brought to the drug users parents and family, living in the hope that tomorrow will be better, which never comes to pass.

A bad situation is established the moment a pusher captivates a potential user and the resulting source of income is established for himself. It all begins with him, the pusher.

The moment a customer is established, a stream of unpleasant events slowly starts to develop in the life of the user.

It is the constant bodily demand for drugs, that the addicted have no control over, that eventually forces the user into a life of crime. In our case, it resulted in the death of our son, due to our antiquated laws, that for one hundred years, we have been using, to deal with this drug problem.

All of the problems that are caused by illegal drug laws, I believe, can be resolved by legalizing them.

We must take a new approach to our drug problem, that has been crushing the lives of so many for so long. With 10% of our population being addicted to drugs, this amounts to approximately 32 million people.

If you assume that all drug addicts have two parents and at least one sibling, on average, then having a drug addict in your family and the affects to all of the people involved, would be an additional 96 million.

If you add the affected family members of the addicted, this would total, close to 128 million of our citizens, or more than 1/3 of our population, that suffer, at any given time, in some form or other, from our nation's drug problems.

I am sure that if we were to decriminalize drugs, and if it is carefully and properly explained to the American public, it would be widely accepted.

Billions of dollars would be saved yearly. Not only by our state and city governments, but for the citizens of this country too. Our crime rate would also be greatly reduced.

Certain steps must be taken. The first step would be to decriminalize the use of drugs completely. We should never give up on the idea of removing drugs from our societies.

However, we cannot ignore the millions of drug users that are reliant on drugs, and the suffering from the detox effect that it will have on them when stopping.

This must strongly be considered. I am sure we could assist them to become free of drugs without pain.

Every state rehabilitation center should be set up with a small medical staff in its employ. The number of centers should be determined, if possible, by estimating how many drug addicts live in each state, and also be inclusive of all of the prisoners that are incarcerated in the city and state jails of each state.

Use the money that would be spent to house a prisoner on average of approximately $44,000 a year per prisoner. It would be used instead to aid addicts to become rehabilitated.

Considering all the money our government spends to keep drugs illegal, that continues years on end, and has been spending for many decades, that did nothing to correct our drug problem.

If the same effort was applied to correcting or legalizing drugs, and started helping the addicts with curing their addiction, we may be able to stop the cost spent on their individual cure.

We could do this in about 30 days or less, or at least bring the cost way down to a reasonable level. It would be less than the costs that our government is spending on having drugs being kept illegal.

If necessary, a small temporary tax could be imposed to assist in payment to implement this drug plan. Inmates that have committed serious crimes that were drug related should remain in jail.

All other non-violent drug crime prisoners should be released to rehabilitation centers to be rehabilitated and to be able to apply for work in their community, and not have to say that they were ever incarcerated.

No one in prison should be released unless they have served a month in prison to guarantee that they have gotten over that detox period. This would shorten their time in rehabilitation considerably.

These centers should also serve as distribution locations, where addicts can obtain drugs free of charge, with certain conditions. They would have to attend classes to help them become normalized citizens of their communities.

The time and length of classes shall be determined by the experienced members of the centers' medical staff. It would and could help if applied to all drug centers throughout the States.

We now have 14,000 rehabilitation centers in the United States at this present time. We know that, to rehabilitate one addict, would take a minimum of 28 days.

With approximately 250 work days in a year, 8 inmates could be helped, if we helped, one at a time, in one year. Having a class of 20, we then could help 160 addicts in one year at one center. Having access to 14,000 centers, in one year we could enroll 2, 520,000 people that are addicted. It would more than cover the 98,500 inmates we currently have in jail now.

These rehabilitation centers then can be used to handle the 32 million, that are receiving free drugs as a reward, for attending classes. By applying the above numbers to the 32 million addicts that are currently in our country, having classes of 20 addicts in all 14000 rehabilitation centers, all 32 million could be handled in about 12 years or less.

We could play with the numbers, increase the size of classes. Changes and improvements over time could be made, as we learn more about how to deal with our drug problems. Cures may come about faster.

But one thing is certain, we will start to take control of our drug problems, to become a drug free nation. The other effects that are married to illegal drugs will subside, giving large savings, in the many areas' related to what once was a necessity, that was brought about with illegal drugs.

The released prisoners have already been detoxed during their time spent in prison. Their classes would be to convince them to remain free of drugs.

I believe, that in most cases, the main reason they return to drugs is because they are continuously being refused decent jobs.

They become driven back on drugs through frustration. If they are drug free, and the stigma of being a criminal is removed, with the proper guidance, they would have a very good chance to turn their life around.

This will prove to be a huge leap forward, in the

life of a once before drug addict. Now they can say no to that one haunting question. Have you ever been incarcerated?

I am sure, that among the many past users of drugs, there can be found many articulate young men and women, with a deep understanding of what goes on in the mind of the addicted. That would be useful to the centers.

Having been on drugs themselves, they would have first-hand knowledge of the chaotic confused mind, that the drug addict deals with constantly. The endless days of suffering, both physical and mental, so very painful to endure, so impossible to cure.

Having been addicted themselves, they would be very understanding. They would be an asset to become any part of a crew working on rehabilitating the men and women seeking to be cured. Lecturing is a very useful tool that can be used effectively.

The government could institute training programs and aptitude tests, that would aid the men and women, in helping them find decent jobs, to become part of the working community.

There remains 32 million people, that are addicted, living in all 50 states. Some may have served time in jail. A high percentage, I imagine, that are 18 years old and younger have not been in prison, to their advantage. All would be entitled to receive free drugs.

Once it is established, that drug use is not a crime, knowing that free drugs can be had, the pressure to the person addicted would immediately subside. The anguish to their whole family will also end.

Their parents especially, would finally have some peace of mind. A return to normal living can be realized once again. If their parents, opening their home's to them until they found work, and were able to support themselves, this can make a huge difference in their recovery.

Automatically, these changes may take place and I believe it would encourage their family to assist in their recovery. To be free of drugs completely is the purpose of this plan. If the understanding is there and there is cooperation from the rest of their family, it would then become an inspirational factor to quicken their recovery.

To be able to do so, they must attend classes that would greatly help them in their goal, to free themselves of their terrible drug habit. A habit that was forced on them, in most cases, now given a chance to, once again, become part of and respected as a part of a community.

A habit that has caused them to lose all that they had ever owned, leaving them to live so miserable a life, alive but not living, lost in the depth of their own terrible situation.

So difficult to be understood by the majority of our society, except for family. Now if we could have a new approach to our drug problem, a new life and a safer environment may now be in sight.

Different programs or classes would be designed, according to the needs of their individual problems. In some cases, have family members involved, that would assist in their recovery.

The approach to the 32 million drug addicts would be a little different. There should never be pressure or forcing anyone to become drug free. It has to be of their own desire, for any plan applied, to be effective.

Classes could be doubled to 20 in a class or more, 20 seems to be an ideal number, but conditions may be a better way of deciding that and other questions that may come about. Most cases, though similar, are not always the same. Therefore, cases should be viewed and dealt with in accordance to their need. A painless detox program would be offered to them.

A slow removal from drugs, a plan designed by

professionals, to ensure that they will have a high percent of success.

The program to detox them, painlessly, that is offered to them, must be administered with the understanding that, under no circumstances, will they be refused the drug that they feel they need.

I feel confident, that if we can gain their trust, we will have them free of drugs in a very short time. Once we have proven to the users that we can help them, I am sure that recruiting them into our program will become easy.

I do believe that a percentage of the 32 million people on drugs in this country, started with experimenting, innocently looking for the high they had heard so much about. Most likely by pushers.

Those with the addictive genes became hooked very easily, and they will be the most difficult to cure, but not impossible to help. It is important to note, that they must want to be helped. That is key to them being cured of their habit.

The others will become clean reasonably quick in my opinion, because most addicts hate the fact they are caught up in drugs but feel helpless, they can see no escape for themselves, to be free. I am sure if a plan is implemented, we can have a significant number of people off drugs in less than three years.

I cannot understand why we have not had any effort to deal with our drug problem in the past. Most of what I researched has proven to me that there are very positive answers to correct this drug situation that confronts us.

Why have we let our citizens suffer with crimes in our neighborhoods, by those with the problem of addiction?

Also, families that have tried their best to deal with this problem for so long, are alone with the family members they care for, while the cost to our government runs into billions of dollars a year. In my opinion, all unnecessary spending of tax payers' money.

Can we realize the tremendous amount of money spent on our drug problem over all of these years? So many areas' to our drug problem, so wide spread that generated unbelievable cost's, to so many.

There are so many advantages to legalizing drugs. This is something we can and should do. Let's stop the suffering to so many of our young citizens and to their families.

Let's stop making them criminals with antiquated laws. Give them a chance in life, also for all of the rest of the addicted in our society.

Why don't we help our own suffering drug population? I think I have outlined the advantages of legalizing drugs very clearly.

My purpose was to bring our drug problem to the surface. It has been a very expensive serious problem, to so many of our people, and it doesn't have to be.

Let me give you an idea of what our saving could amount to. How we would have enough money to spend on all the costs involved with legalizing drugs, including the full cost of the rehabilitation centers.

This would mean having a staff, food, medical supplies, anything that would be needed to have this plan succeed.

These costs will only be for less than a dozen years at most. After that, the length of time needed, to keep these centers open, would become negligible.

Realize that we have been spending huge amounts of money on this, our drug problem for the last one hundred years.

Now, for only the next 12 years of what might be a slight increase in spending, we then can see an end to our spending and also to our serious drug problems. I came across this while using AOL search, here is the report that I found.

Estimated Savings from Legalizing Drugs

The report estimates that legalizing drugs saves about 48.8 billion dollars a year in government spending on prohibition. $33.1 billion of this saving would accrue to states and local governments, while $15.7 billion would accrue to Federal Government.

Approximately $13.7 billion of savings would result from the legalization of marijuana. $22.3 billion from the legalization of Cocaine and Heroin and $12.8 billion from legalization of all other drugs.

Imagine almost 97.6 billion dollars a year. This is what we are spending a year on our drug problem, here in our country. Plus, the $44,000 a year cost per prisoner. Year after year, for the many years of our citizens living with this problem, and our government didn't take steps to correct it.

We have been spending this large amount of money on drugs, so the money is there, it is available, only we have been spending it the wrong way.

There is enough money available that if necessary if some of the addicted live to far from the rehabilitation centers, we could afford to find places for them to stay till they have completed their treatment. Possibly the centers could house them as inpatients.

I do realize that there may be questions or details to legalizing drugs that I am not aware of. I am sure we can find the answer to any question that might arise.

We need to organize a special committee to lay out plans and formulate a recovery procedure to follow as a nationwide project, that interacts with rehabilitation centers in all other states, to be able to have an exchange of ideas.

I want to be clear about the amount of centers needed. The 14,000 rehabilitation centers we use now, is the amount that we have available to us. If we use them efficiently, to establish how many centers we might need, we can possibly, over time, operate with fewer centers and accomplish the same results. Over time, we will slowly eliminate the rehabilitation centers completely.

As it stands now, here across the United States, there are approximately 14,000 rehabilitation centers, with the number growing by an unnecessary amount, that are mostly subsidized by our government.

To reach all the addicted patients, I imagine, we would not need more rehabilitation centers than the ones we already have.

The idea is that we can get control of our countries drug problem with little effort. A problem that I do see is that with centers spread over this vast area of our country and dealing with the mind of the unfortunate drug addict, few might make it to a facility to receive help.

A simpler approach that might be more cost effective, I would suggest, is using local hospitals, along with the centers we have available. We could work out a plan to treat the addicts as outpatients with some as inpatients, so as to treat them according to their needs.

As the amount of addicts diminish, the hospitals would be used as a permanent place to treat addicts and eliminate the drug centers completely.

The key to having successful results, is first to decriminalize the use of all drugs. Also, that the addicted should not have to pay for their supply of drugs.

This would eliminate all drug pushers and cartels immediately. Imagine stopping them dead in their tracks, forcing them completely out of business.

This alone, I feel is a good reason to legalize drugs. The big gain is, what it will do, for so many citizens, that really suffer severely with their addiction. We would be fair in saying, that all members of a family, that has someone with a drug problem living with them, are forced to live with tremendous pressure and strain.

This is put upon them because of our unnecessary, unreasonable laws. Unless you are living, or have lived with a drug addict, in your home, it is impossible to feel the suffering and hurt the entire family is unfairly put through. And it is constant, there is no relief from the stress apply to you or the other love ones in your household.

This is what takes place in any family where a member comes down with a serious illness like heart failure or cancer, it causes family members to become deeply involved. With having this illness that is drug related, the involvement also becomes greatly increased.

The addicted, if they are at home or not, there is no escaping the whirlpool that your mind is put through. When they are at home, most times you cannot satisfy their need.

When they leave the safety of your home, there is a momentary sigh of relief as the calm replaces the turmoil that they always bring with them. Then, fear sets in that something bad will happen to them, knowing the state of mind they are living with.

Your lives have become completely absorbed in the world of the user. Actually, they have taken complete control of your life. As a parent you cannot walk away from it.

This is not a temporary situation. This has been a daily happening that has been ongoing for years, and in some cases, going on and off for decades.

There are 32 million addicts caught up in and living this terrible, uncontrollable life. If so, we can realize that with having mothers and fathers possibly brothers and sisters, the number of people affected could easily become 120 to 150 million people, more or less, that are caused to suffer.

Most would be innocently involved. How can we stand by and have this happen in our free country? Those implicated are caught in a web, 150 million people have lost their freedom, trapped as they may be, because, bound to the families of those addicted, only can they be free, if drugs are legalized.

In Summary

Our country has proven, that in the last 240 years, that it is old and has been finally organized as a nation. That we, the United States of America, have been forced to deal with and overcame many obstacles in our past. Many times over, we have been challenged, and responded adequately to the problems that we were faced with.

America is a resilient nation. When faced with danger, because of our independent nature, we are very capable to rise above any problems that may confront us.

And now, once again, we are up against three major problems here at home. The problems that we must deal with, is not to help other countries. We are seriously faced with our own problems and it is time to help ourselves.

I would like to see all of our service personnel with their families, that are spread throughout the world, brought back home to America. Let them be placed on our northern and southern boarders as our fence is being built in the south. Not all, but most, that would join a sizable force already in place to assure our boarders will finally be secure.

The democratic liberals, have little or no interest at

all, in securing our borders for several reasons.

They are willing to spend as much money as they can, giving the illegal immigrants all the benefits that the natural citizens of this nation receive, using our tax dollars. This will guarantee more support for the democrats.

To have more people relying on our government, enables the democrats to gain more power. It also eases the changeover to socialism, when the majority of people of a nation becomes reliant on government. We must take strong measures to stop the influx of immigrants entering our country.

We know this is what our present administration refuses to do. It seems as though, what is good for America, is never good for him. He is now in France talking about Global Warming.

He joined together with over 195 countries and 150 world leaders to talk about HOT AIR, while the POTUS and his crew, are ignoring the fact, that Isis is setting the world on fire.

There is never any talk of the thousands of people, running for their lives, to escape the onslaught of Isis, looking to cut the throats of Christians.

Global warming is prime in the mind of our leader only now after cells, in Paris, killed and wounded so many innocent people, and have now done the same in California. I agree with Mr. Trump when he commented "How ridiculous".

I also agree with him, to hit them, Isis, really hard, by defeating them completely on the battle field. Any cells they have in place in the USA or elsewhere in the world, would then be stranded. It would minimize our fight against them. It would demoralize them, removing their will to fight.

I would start a systematic surveillance of all Mosque's in our country, looking for cells, but realizing that there are also many friendly Muslim's that would not bring harm to us.

However, they must be made to understand that if there is nothing to hide, then they have nothing to fear. What we are doing, is to make the country that they chose to make their home, a safer place for them to live in also.

Oil fields! I would not bomb the oil fields, but I would bomb the hell out of any truck, train or any vehicular transporter of oil they have.

Then send an over whelming number of our best fighters, into the oil fields to secure them totally.

We should claim the rights to the oil fields, to help pay for the war we are fighting, that they brought against us.

If we use the full power of our forces and having a strong coalition of our allies fight along with us.

We, with the nations involved, should have all our Generals, organize a plan to carry out this war.

I have no doubt that we would defeat these terrorists very quickly. I am sure the world will start looking at us with respect and we, with a strong honest leader, could then realize our greatness once again. We have lost so much respect over the last seven years, under this present, democratic administration.

Our United States, still has a sad problem with citizens that are suffering from drug addiction. I still hope that our leaders would think about all of us, that are not on drugs, but are caused to suffer as a result of drugs, because we live in close contact with an addicted person.

I cannot express enough, how penetrating, into the mind and souls of parents and other loved ones it becomes. How helpless a situation you are faced with and the awful way it effects your entire life.

This is no way that we should be forced to live, but we are, especially if you are poor. The effect of illegal drugs on Americans, that live under the poverty line, multiplies itself many fold. What happens to the families of addicts because of their addiction is never talked about, or even considered by law enforcers, or law makers.

I have tried to show earlier, how so many lives are impacted, if we continue to not change our drug laws. I strongly believe that a President would gain strength among the people, if he tackled the drug problems of this nation. Having a third of our population, at a minimum of 120 million or more people, severely suffering, as a result of not having drugs legalized.

We have been fighting a war against drugs, that has been going on for 100 years or more. We are not winning this war. Since this war started, there has not been any signs of improvement.

If we take a good look back into the long history of our drug problem in our nation, show me where there have been any improvements? There isn't any, it is just getting worse.

So isn't it about time to start rethinking what we are doing? Do we want to just continue arresting drug addicts, instead of helping them? I think the time has come, for a new approach to this major problem, which should and must be made, so that the innocent citizens of our nation, that are caught in a bind, are relieved of the bind they are in and get back to a normal life.

If all efforts applied over many decades, do not improve a situation, if there are no satisfactory results, giving relief or hope to the victims of an ongoing tragedy, wouldn't it be time to try something new? I feel that a new approach is called for. I think to legalize drugs, here in America, is long overdue.

I have been writing about the problems that the United States is facing, in the hope that I can have our citizens become aware of the dangers that lie ahead.

If an effort is in the making, to have our country restore the greatness it once had, one of our priorities must be to have an answer to the suffering of over 120 million poor people caught in this cycle.

Imagine that more than one third of the people of our nation, have no way of correcting their situation, once a member of their family becomes addicted. Only through legalizing drugs can we put an end to their suffering. Only through our government, can the proper action be taken.

In my opinion, this is a very solvable problem. Try to realize that people of wealth do not suffer when they become addicted. It is only the poor families of the addicted, and the addicted themselves, that go through enormous hardship.

We must be made to live through this very unpleasant experience to have a feel for the importance of solving this serious problem, that has been with us for so many long years.

All of the serious obstacles that our nation faces are secondary to what has been happening in our country at the hands of the Fabian Societies' progressive movement.

If we do not face and stop this movement now, if we don't make this our first priority, if we become a socialist country, then the greatness of America will be lost forever. Brute force will become the laws that govern our, once free, nation.

This very important priority should be taking place in our country, to stop the Fabian Society before it is too late. It is so hard to get people to believe, that this movement is real, and is happening now in our country, and has happened already in all of Europe and Great Britain.

Our president, Ronald Reagan, must have had concerns of this great nation losing its freedom. He, like so many others, saw a strong move to the left taking place in our country, and could not understand why.

He must have not known of the Fabian Society, or of the idea of world dominance, that has been their plan, since 1884, or of their relentless effort to steal our freedom, and how secretly they have advanced this idea, to where it is now, very close to completion.

What they have in store for America, to socialize our nation, can and will happen, if America does not unify to defeat this organization. The people of this great young nation has yet to reach its full potential, when change began to take place.

It was the end of the first world war when they started to infiltrate into our government. We must not let this happen. We cannot let our people, become the victims of the Fabian society, now or ever.

Our goal should be to convince the leaders of socialist nations in this world, to free their people. Instead, we stand to be convinced by the liberals to becoming socialized. We must realize what is taking place in our nation to save our country.

President Reagan must of had a sense or fear of our freedom being lost when he wrote these words of wisdom, in an effort to have us realize a danger, that we one day might face.

He said and I quote:

"Freedom is never more than one generation away from extinction. We didn't pass it on to our children in the blood stream. It must be fought for, protected and handed on to them to do the same. Or one day we will spend our sunset years telling our children and our children's children, what it was once like in the United States, where men were free."

Ronald Reagan

The United States is in need of a strong, straight forward, president. A man with integrity, honest to himself and to the public that he represents. A president that is proud, firm and honest, at all times, especially when dealing with other nations of this world, so that he is trusted and believed by our friends and enemies alike.

Our America must gain the honor and respect it once had, to become the great nation we once were.

The people of this great nation, felt that sense of being proud to be an American, when President Reagan was at the helm.

But soon after, think about what the Clinton's brought to the White House. Selling Lincoln's bedroom to visitors from Hollywood, selling our government computers as scrap to China by the car load.

How much information was there for the Chinese to learn about us? How about his reputation with women?

Are we now to consider having Hillary Clinton in charge of our America?

She cannot make a speech without her embellishing it with a falsehood. Nothing is ever her fault. She can always find a video to blame. Do we want to listen to four or eight years of blame and lies?

We are comparatively, a young nation, yet the most advanced, strongest, and freest country in the world.

I cannot say we are the safest country, because we are not. This is where our problems arise. Where can I find the words needed, to convince this nation that it is facing a serious problem?

A problem with an enemy, that has been at work, slowly destroying us, for the last 100 years or more, using lobbyists and various unions and organizations, that were formed by the Fabian progressives, to take control of this nation.

They have had one objective in mind, with a plan that they have, to make the United States part of a world order, based on a socialist ideology.

Take away our Republic, remove from us, the

American people, our Bill of Rights and our Constitution. Take away the freedom that our forefathers gave to us and replace it with a dictatorial government, to have our nation change over to socialism.

The people of this world, although they are in awe of America, they are also jealous of the freedom that thrives in the United States of America.

If a King or Queen rules the land, the people are not free. If you live under communism, the people are not free. If you live as a socialist, or any other form of government other than a Republic, the people are not free. Billions of humans living on this earth, sadly, live in fear of their governments.

We, the people of our free nation, sometimes find it difficult to understand how fortunate we are to live in a country like ours. People around the world may understand better than we do, how great it must be to have the free society that we live in.

A free society, as outlined in our constitution, that great, honest, caring men, gave to all Americans, so many years ago. Words of wisdom, that remained alive in the hearts of all mankind, and also those living in this country to this day.

We sometimes forget how wonderful a gift it is,

that was given to all American's. True freedom, that no others living on this earth have.

They have little chance in being able to influence their government to see the benefits that could be gained by having freedom for their citizens.

I marvel at the wisdom that the framers of our constitution had. The simple idea of taking away power from a government and giving it to the people.

With that thought in mind, they set in motion a well-planned set of laws, for our nation to follow.

A Constitution and a Bill of Rights, that has served American's well for the last 240 years. For over the last 120 years, our Constitution and the laws that bind it, have slowly been discredited. Our Republic, like our American Flag, has been trampled on by those on the progressive left.

A strong effort to change our nation over to socialism is the goal of the liberal democrats or the progressives, as Hillary and President Obama like to be called.

They, having been the pawns of the Fabian progressive society, are close to achieving what they had set out to do to us, so many long years ago.

Their goal was to change our Republic to Socialism.

What seemed to be so impossible so many years past, is now what has become extremely real, made possible, only because it is so difficult to convince anyone of this movement, that is taking place in our country.

The Fabian Society's approach to secretly and slowly penetrate into every branch of our government, has been working for the progressive movement quite efficiently.

They have a strong influence in the Board of Education, through unions that they have formed, and the many organizations that I have mentioned earlier.

Although having control, they have never made themselves spread too thin.

Instead, they have gained strength, having been slow in their development, over the long years that they were in the making, well established, with a deliberate plan, patiently carried out over decades, to conquer America.

You cannot win a battle, if you cannot see who you are fighting. This has been the problem that we have been facing for the last 100 years or more.

When I ask the question of most people that I know, did you ever hear of the Fabian Society, the answer is NO, 99% of the time. And they show no interest in knowing who they are, as though frightened by the very truth of their existence.

This is the very reason they, the Fabian Society, have become so powerful. It is because nobody wants to believe that they exist, or that they are the reason why, the United States is now leaning so far to the left.

They are able to conquer undisturbed, in their quest of world dominance, by operating under the cover of secrecy.

We are on the verge of losing our freedom! It is happening now! The door is ready to close, to slam shut on our freedom forever, if another liberal progressive person becomes our next president.

We cannot let another Liberal Administration, be in control of our destiny.

What the Fabian Society have in mind for the people of our nation, is to take away our freedom. If they succeed, over time, what America once was, will not be remembered.

Once the people of a nation loses their right to a voice in the place where they live, in reality, they have lost their country. They have become a people without a nation.

Take a serious look at the economy of Russia and of Cuba, it is a mess.

What is happening in the United States, came about to give power to the few that would be in charge of this once great nation. The oppression that is sure to follow will be real and everlasting.

We will have a huge government controlling the people. Sadly, the citizens of this country will have lost their freedom and be left with no voice at all.

Our coming election is crucial to what may happen next in our country. If we elect an administration, that duplicates what we have now, then the changeover to socialism will follow soon after.

The flame that gave us the glow of greatness, that was alive in the hearts of American's, that the United States has always presented to the world, has been reduced to an ember by our current administration.

We once were an inspirational spark that lit the fire in the hearts and minds of the oppressed people of this world. In the hope that they too, one day, could reach our shores and bask in the greatness, that America has always symbolized.

That to become an American, was more than a desire, it was a dream that brought great men and women to this land of ours. When you free the man, you free the minds of mankind, and great ideas can be born, as I believe was brought out in the minds of the framers of our Constitution.

They were great men, with a great idea, that was never tried by any nation before, in the history of this world.

A Bill of Rights, also by their design, to ensure that its laws would guarantee that our Constitution be followed, that would keep our great nation on this path to freedom.

An idea that was simple and profound, precisely formed, 240 years ago. An idea that people born into a new born nation, in order to become completely free, the people should be in control of the government.

Great men could rise out of a need of a troubled nation to resolve itself.

These are my perceptions, of what I see is happening to this nation of ours. This surge to the left is not happening because there is a need to improve our life style, as candidates like Bernie Sanders and Hillary Clinton, would want us to believe.

It is a plan, by design, over many decades, **to socialize America.**

I have seen this developing over the 87 years of my life. I felt a need to inform anyone who would take the time to share my thoughts.

For all of you who have, I am humbly thankful.

May God Bless you! And may God Bless America!